"For over thirty-fiv[e] teachers in America, [Andy] [pro]duced sounds from me that I have been waiting for all my life to make."

—*Jose Ferrer*

"Andy sings the words like Frank Sinatra does."

—Julie Harris

"Andy is the male Barbra Streisand."

—*Phyllis Diller*

"My daughter wrote a song when she was 11. She told me that Andy was in her thoughts when she composed it. Nothing captures Andy's spirit better.

> *Ring of Light*
> How do you find a true friend
> A person with you 'til the bitter end
> The world, the life, the sun, it seems to shine
>
> A ring of golden light surrounds me
> It seems to wrap right up around me
> Whenever I'm with you, it shines
> The ring of light."

—*Paul Tudor Jones II*

"Andy Anselmo has brought joy to thousands of lives through the wonder of music over six decades. These pages bring those experiences to life."

—*Stanley F. Druckenmiller*

When you're studying, you want to learn and get better, but you also want to feel as though you're in a safe place that no one is going to drag you down or tell you that everything you're doing is wrong or be overly negative in any way. I know when I go to the Singer's Forum every week for my lesson that it's going to be a great experience, that I'm going to walk out of there feeling better, whether or not I sang particularly well. It's that encouragement and positivity—the good vibe I get from Andy and everyone there—that keeps me returning week after week. It's good."

—*Billy Stritch*

"Andy Anselmo is a star. Not only a star in the sense that God gave him amazing musical talent and inner beauty, but star in the sense that he guides those in the dark and gives off light to all those around him, even in the darkest times. 'To the world you might be one person, but to one person you might be the world.' (Anonymous) The previous quote pretty much sums up how much Andy means to me, and I am confident that his star quality, compassion, and loving heart has left a mark on the world of music and everyone he has known."

—*Caroline Jones*

"When I got the part of Che in Evita I turned to Andy, and said: 'Can you make me strong and teach me how not to hurt myself?' He did just that, and 25 years later it's still working. Andy, thank you, thank you, thank you."

Love,
—*Mandy Patinkin*

"It's always a pleasure to work with Andy, who was my vocal coach at the Strasberg Institute 25 years ago, and is one of the greatest teachers in the world."

—*Alec Baldwin*

"Spend time with Andy and you will invariably feel better about your voice, your self, and unaccountably, the world in general. He lifts your voice, he lifts your spirits."

—*Amanda Green*

"Andy—I experienced him not only as a talented and uplifting teacher, but as a noble warrior who conquered the demons of his past; emerging spiritually into a garden of flowers with a plethora of scents that sweeten his present and the lives of all those whom he touches."

—*Anita Treinkman*

"I'd always wanted to sing but thought there was no way I could. But with Andy's teaching, I now have a singing art that still stays in perfect order. I'm performing all over the country with 'Street Songs,' and even in the White House, and it's all entirely his doing. If I were to wish for something to happen to someone that I love, I'd wish that at some time in their life, they would be this lucky. I love him very much."

—*Geraldine Fitzgerald*

A Star-Crossed Life
A Memoir

Andy Anselmo with
Eileen Dolen Newman

VANTAGE PRESS
New York

FIRST EDITION

Published by Vantage Press, Inc.
419 Park Ave. South, New York, NY 10016

Manufactured in the United States of America
ISBN: 0-533-14926-6

Library of Congress Catalog Card No.: 2004092805

0 9 8 7 6 5 4 3 2 1

Contents

Prologue

My maternal grandfather's farm, outside of Brocton, New York on the shore of Lake Erie, had been in my family since 1901. I fell in love with the farm from the moment of my first awareness of it. My affection for it has grown ever since. It's in my thoughts constantly. It represents peace, tranquility and so much love. My grandfather raised grapes on that farm and I can remember spending all my vacations and summers with him and my step-grandmother. They were so much older than I was but we communicated on some level. I adored my grandfather. He made me feel special and, as I was his only child's first-born child, he doted on me.

I remember helping to tie the grapes in the spring, and making wine in the fall. There were animals all over the place, chickens, pigs, dogs, cats, horses who did the plowing and even drove us to town. My favorite horse was named Queenie. She was all white and beautiful. I looked forward to riding her to pasture every evening. My father, an upholsterer, made a saddle for me and I rode on that horse as proud as I could be.

I called the farm my summer home. It made me feel rich though we didn't have much money. It was during the Great Depression that I grew up. It was such a different time. People today could never envision it. But I refused to see our poverty, and I concentrated on my singing and music to get me through the sad times. That is why the farm meant so much to me. I had a place to go on weekends, vacations and summers. I made the farm sound more glamorous than it was to my friends because I wanted them to think I had as much as they did. I don't think it was wrong. I had to survive somehow.

I looked forward to getting up into our buggy with the fringe on top and to riding with grandfather to town for groceries and whatever else we needed. Now it's easy for me to sing that pretty song from *Oklahoma!* "The Surrey With The Fringe On The Top." We were probably the only people around still holding on to the past. We made our way bravely into town with all eyes looking at us as we went from place to place. Now, when I see dignitaries driving along with the top down and waving, I know exactly how they feel, but I know I felt better than they do. You see, I was with my dear grandfather and my horse and I was carrying my whole world with me. I was happy. What more did I need?

We faced the world together, all of us, even when we brought the grapes to the processing factory to sell. I dreaded the moment of inspection of the grapes because it would make my grandfather either happy or sad. When the price wasn't right, we would drive home sadly, my grandfather hardly speaking. I would hate those people for making him sad, and looked forward to when he would be himself again.

I never lost my excitement when I knew I was going back to my grandfather's house. That excitement persists even to this day. I still expect Grandfather to come out of the house to greet me, and my beautiful step-grandmother, with her white hair piled high on her head, rushing out, always with her apron on. My mother and father would happily leave me there, knowing how I felt about the farm.

Then again I looked forward to when they would

return, because sometimes I would feel very lonely. Books were my friends and I read voraciously, everything I could find. We had a fine library out there in Brocton and I saw a great deal of it.

When it was time to return to Buffalo, I knew my grandparents would be lonely without me. The winters were long then, with tremendous snowfalls, but no matter what, my grandfather and I would go out into the woods to cut the Christmas tree. I was happy doing that and we would return home to decorate it, then sing around the tree. Some years the trees were better than other years, but we would pretend it was beautiful and decorate it as best we could.

Now that they are gone, I can still see them around the house, doing all the chores. I feel their presence. That part of me will always stay young, for when I arrive at the farm, I feel young again, and I remember things as they were with those loving people, the likes of whom I will never see again.

You see, I had a summer house and I was special. I was somebody very rich, for it is the simple things that make us rich and happy. And I have those memories with me, always.

I

Family

My paternal grandfather, Santo Anselmo, who lived with us and for whom I was named, was very different from my maternal grandfather, Giacomo DiPasquale. They both came from the same town in Sicily, Monte Maggiore Bel Sito. Grandfather Santo was very old-world Sicilian, patriarchal. He had done very well here and he was very good-looking. I remember him pretty well. He absolutely adored me. I was his first grandson and was named for him, so I was *it*. My father, Angelo Anselmo, was one of twins. They thought at birth that Angelo was going to be the one to die, but it turned out the other twin died. When my paternal grandmother died, my father was about eight or nine. I think it's where my father's headaches came from, living with my grandfather, who was a tough taskmaster. Grandfather Anselmo did not remarry. There were five or six other children and an aunt who was with them until she got married. But my father spent some years with my grandfather, by himself.

Then, when my mother and father were married, Grandfather Santo came to live with them, not the best thing for a young marriage.

I remember when they had guests, at nine o'clock he'd get up and say, "Okay, everybody go home. I have to go to bed now." To him, it was not their home, it was his. Some of this came up in my therapy, sixty years later! But when I was born, he was just so happy. I think he died when I was about six or seven. I vaguely remember he looked like a very big man to a little boy. Grandfather Santo was very imposing. That "Toscanini" look, ferocious, that's the look. That was the temperament, too. He owned real estate. He bought and sold houses. He was rich, not rich-rich, but he had money, and, of course, all his children were wondering who was going to get it. If anybody should have, it was my father and mother, because they put up with him for all those years.

But it didn't work out that way. One uncle was married to a woman who was a complete neurotic, and sharp where the others were not. She wanted to see to it that she got more than anybody else got. My mother was naïve. She was not smart that way. And this lady got my grandfather away from our house at a time when he was ill, and then had him change his will. Everyone suspected it might happen, but it was still unbelievable when it did. So the others did not get much and she and her husband got most of the money and property.

And by then, money really mattered a lot. The Depression had taken hold and along with the lives of millions of others, it changed our lives, too.

In our household, my mother probably was, in a sense, more influential than my father. He was a great disciplinarian, I mean, he appeared strong and was the man of the house, but as I look at it now, my mother, in her own way, got her own way. She seemed more passive and easy going, but as I looked at her in later life, I could see that she really ran things.

You don't meet a man like my father every day. He was fabulous. And giving, very giving. If he had two cents and you needed it, he'd give it to you. He was so generous. He was amazing. He never made you feel poor. He'd always come home with a little bag of sweets. If he went out, he came back remembering us with something. It might be a piece of candy, but he never came home empty-handed. And this was when he didn't have any money. But he never made you feel you didn't have it.

We always ate well. My mother was a good cook and we always had company. I don't remember when our house wasn't full of people. The coffee pot was always on. My father would go to get special doughnuts. I'd ride with him and we'd go to Freddy's and bring the doughnuts back and everyone would sit around and have doughnuts and coffee.

My father never over-ate. He maintained his body-weight till the day he died. He didn't gain five pounds in all the years he lived. He knew when to stop and never took a second helping. He had beautiful green eyes, dark hair and a strawberry blond moustache. Red hair ran in his family. He was very muscular. He was a cross between Gilbert Roland, Errol Flynn and Ronald Colman. He had that kind of look.

When he died, he was sixty. The carotid arteries in his neck were blocked. He had surgery on one side and then, three years later, did the other side, but it didn't work. He went into a coma and after about a week, he died. He had been getting periods of blindness and had other problems. It would not have been much of a life for him. He had been a runner, a baseball player and a champion bridge player all his life.

My mother, my sisters, Annetta and Carolyn, and I grieved for him for a long time. He lived to see his grand-child—my sister Carolyn's son, Jeff. That child made a great difference to my mother and Carolyn. He brought them a lot of joy. Mother would sing to him and he'd laugh and wave his arms and legs. That was her therapy. She had to smile at him, this little baby, looking at her, laughing. How could she sit there and cry? Jeff's a lawyer now, and he still has that happy disposition.

The only arguments my parents had were about money. There never seemed to be enough money. I think my feelings about money came from that period when I had to worry about it so much. Money, or the lack of it, caused so much unhappiness.

I know it left a mark because my parents chickened out when we couldn't pay the rent. I was the one who always had to go to the landlady and tell her that we would be late with the rent. I was only a kid, ten, eleven, twelve. That they would let me do it was, I think, horrible, as I look back on it. I was the one who had to face this woman. She was a "Mrs. Danvers" type. You know what I mean. She'd stand there in the doorway. She would hardly even open the door. I would look up at her and say, "Mrs. Muscato, we can't pay you this week. We'll pay you in two weeks." I would be the one to have to do that. But I seemed to be the strong one, even as a kid. I seemed to have the ability to face up to and talk to people and express myself and have the guts to do it. They didn't realize what it must have been doing to me. That was not a nice thing for any kid. It was terrible. But they couldn't do it. They always asked me to do it. I never refused. In some way, I knew I had to do it, that they couldn't face it, that it was just too humiliating for them. And I wasn't thinking about how humiliating it was for me. I just didn't like to see my parents in that situation, so if I could make it easier, I would.

My sisters tell me that they never felt the pain of being poor because I never let them feel it. I was the oldest. I felt responsible for their happiness. I think it's where I get my imagination from. I elaborated on everything so we wouldn't be "poor." They had no idea we really were poor because I always made them feel like we had everything. It was fun. I made it fun for them and for my parents.

I think a big part of it was my singing. It was a lot of fun for them to go and hear me sing and take all the neighbors and the relatives. It was almost the only fun they had. We had no money. We couldn't go out to restaurants.

I did go to the five-cent movies with my Aunt Mamie. I still adore her. She was over a hundred years old when she died and her mind was sharp. Her legs were weak and she had to walk carefully, but outside of that, she was in great shape. She knew I loved movies and she did, too, so she'd always take me. That was my escape from what was happening.

I think I had to create my life early, the way I wanted it to be. Because it was not pleasant. So I guess that's how I learned to visualize, very early. I visualized it the way I wanted it to be, instead of the way it was. I didn't know how powerful that was, but it got me into a whole life that was wonderful. I didn't feel that poorness then and I began to express myself. I knew I had something and that it was going to pay off. I was going to earn a lot of money. Even though I hated money, I was going to make it because I never wanted to feel poor again. I could never endure feeling poor again. It would be devastating.

So I've tried to insure that I won't feel poor by creating an atmosphere of abundance and opulence around me, as much as I can. When I used to go to the farm, I would feel richer there, even though Grandfather Giacomo and step-grandmother Caterina were poor, too. After all, it was the country. It was just ten acres but it was worked as a real farm. He worked for the railroad, so

9

it was really a weekend thing for him. He had been born on a farm in Sicily so it gave him an opportunity to do the things he enjoyed. He raised grapes and we had a cherry orchard. There was another, smaller, apple orchard. We had the most fantastic vegetable garden you've ever seen: tomatoes, lettuce, cucumbers, onions, corn, peas, eggplant, potatoes, everything. We had pear trees and plum trees, too. It was a spectacular little farm. In the spring, when they would tie the grapes, we'd all go out and help. I don't know how much I did but I was there. And then we would go out to help pick the grapes.

So I had a country house, and my Di Pasquale grandparents were wonderful.

Grandfather Giacomo was a shepherd before he came to America. He would be gone weeks and months at a time, by himself. He spent a lot of time alone, as a young man, which is strange, today. He was alone most of the year. He only saw people when he brought the sheep in for shearing, or at lambing time. I knew he had problems; he would have to take his plate and go outside and sit under a tree when the company got too much for him. He had so many years of that kind of isolation. All the relatives would come in summertime, and that's when he was used to being alone.

Grandfather Giacomo had a brother and a sister, and they owned a large farm in Sicily. The priest was the only one who could read and write, the only one who was educated. I was told that when my grandfather left for America, he could have held on to his share of that property but the priest somehow turned it around and influenced him to give it to the Church because he wouldn't be coming back to Sicily. The priests preyed on people like him, who did not have an education.

That was the story I heard as a boy. When I went to

Sicily, in 1998, I found out Grandfather had given his share of the place to his sister. I went to the farm and it is beautiful. This was my mother's father's family's land.

The farm in Brocton will have been in our family for a hundred years in 2001. Grandfather bought it when he came here, so he must have brought some money with him. He saved it somehow, I don't know how. He was just a farmer and a shepherd boy. Maybe he never spent any money.

There was great drama in my mother's early life. She was the object of a long-running custody battle between her father and her mother's mother, Maria Giallombardo Clement. Maria Clement was very well-to-do. She lived in Westfield, a nearby town. My mother's mother, Nina (Clement) Di Pasquale, died when mother was two years old, giving birth to their second child, a son, who also died. My mother always had love that you cannot imagine from her father. He had adored her mother so. And it was a love that these two people had that was unique at that time. Grandpa was nearly seventeen years older than my mother's mother when they married. When my grandmother died, my grandfather was devastated. Naturally, at that time, my mother stayed with the Clements. And they adored her, too.

So mother was reared by her maternal grandmother from the age of two, and by her mother's brothers and sisters. One of her mother's brothers had been a fruit peddler and as a young man had been shot dead by a rival peddler for being on the wrong side of the street. That tragedy marked the whole Clement family. When Nina, my grandmother, died, they were all single and they had a little money. They were not poor.

So, when my grandfather remarried, maybe a year and a half or two years later, he wanted mother back and the Clements didn't want to give her up. They were afraid that Caterina, her new stepmother, might be mean. Old Mrs. Clement, my great-grandmother, had had a stepmother who was mean and she knew what a mean stepmother could do to a child. And you've got to remember, my grandfather couldn't read or write. But he took her to court to get my mother back. It was like the Gloria Vanderbilt case. He said, "She's my daughter and I'm raising her." And that was it. The Clements had money to fight for her. They owned a factory and lived very nicely. Then old Mrs. Clement charged my grandfather child support for all the time my mother had been with her. Great-grandmother Clement thought that would discourage him because he had to pay it all at once, but he came up with it. He was working for the railroad and had saved every penny he could. He said, "If I have to sell my farm, I'll get my daughter back." And he paid her. But they were always good friends, even after all that.

My step-grandmother, Caterina, was a nice lady. When my mother went to live with them, she must have been about four years old. Grandfather would come home from work and he would examine my mother every night to see she didn't have any bruises or sores. And every night he would say to her, "How was your day? Did anything happen that I should know about?" Every night, he quizzed her because he knew the Clements would take her back if they could. He would lose her.

My mother had such love all the time from her grandmother, aunts, uncles, her father and her stepmother, so she had a lot of love to give her own family. She was blonde until she was seventeen when she caught the influenza that killed millions. She survived. Her hair fell out and grew back, but it was brown. There is no record of her real birthday. The church where she was baptized burned down when she was very young. Her mother died when she was one and a half or two. She said her name was Loretta but my sister, Carolyn, says it was Lucrezia. Mom hated that name and liked a woman she knew whose name was Loretta. Her father and everyone else called her "Fifi." When he took her to be enrolled in kindergarten, he probably said, "This is '*ma figlia*,'" (my daughter) and the WASP teacher thought he said something like "Fifi" and put her name down that way. In 1943, when she needed a Social Security number, she and her father had to go to Albany to get a record of her birth. That's probably when Carolyn heard her real name, Lucrezia.

I remember how she and my father would discipline us. Actually, my father would do it. We'd have to sit in a dining room chair, the one with arms, in the middle of the room, and everybody was to ignore us. We were never sent to our bedrooms or put somewhere alone or facing the wall. They didn't believe in sending a child off alone to feel sorry for himself, or get mad. No way. We'd sit in that dining room chair, the one with arms, and we were not supposed to speak, or be spoken to.

It was so funny. My sisters would never stop talking when they were in the chair. I was supposed to go by and ignore them. That was the punishment. You'd have to sit there for maybe half an hour. Then you got up and it was all over.

You had to have done something serious, like being disobedient, and my father would be trying to get his point across. Or we hadn't eaten something because we didn't like it. Of course, he would eat it just to show us. He didn't like those vegetables but he ate them because he didn't want us to say, "You don't eat them!" My sisters used to giggle a lot. I did, too. We always laughed at our dinner table. My father couldn't understand what was so funny. I used to sit across from my sister, Carolyn, and she would giggle very easily and she made me laugh every time. She still makes me laugh.

We were never spanked. Never. That was our only punishment, not talking. That was a real punishment for me. But Carolyn wouldn't shut up, and Dad would say to my mother, "Is she ever going to be quiet?" My poor dad. At one time or another, we all ended up in that chair. I think it was my mother's idea.

She was loved a lot and she gave us love. Carolyn once told me that in Italian families, brothers, older brothers, were kind of in charge. Well, not in our house. I was a brother. I was not a person who could tell her what to do. My mom and dad were the heads of the house. That was it. When Carolyn was little, going to school, some girls would say how they hated their brothers because they were mean, always bossing, even hitting them. She would say, "Gee, my brother doesn't do that." We weren't raised that way.

I was always very proud of my sisters. I would take them everywhere. I still am and I still do.

II

Buffalo

I was born in Buffalo, New York, on Fargo Street. We
lived upstairs, and there was a family that lived downstairs, named Termini. I don't think it was my Grandfather Anselmo's property, even though he was living with
us at the time and he did own several houses.

The Terminis had a daughter, an adult, probably in
her twenties, by the name of Millie. They also had a piano
and Millie was a terrific pianist. And she was pretty. She
was very pretty.

When I was about three years old, I was really taken
with Millie and the piano. I must have been hearing it
from the day I was born. She would play by the hour,
mostly popular music. And I always wanted to go downstairs; my mother had a difficult time keeping me
upstairs. I always wanted to go downstairs when I heard
the piano, so sometimes she would let me go down and
Millie would let me sit there. And I would be very quiet. I
would just sit there and listen to her. This is how I
learned to listen to students, I guess. I would just sit
there and listen to Millie play. I was in seventh heaven.
This went on for several years. We didn't move from there
until I was six or seven. And I was just taken with Millie
and that piano, and I know it had a lot to do with my
musical life because I had the inclination and she was
there and she was so interesting, I thought. I probably

had a crush on her. I always wanted to go downstairs. And she was wonderful. I would just sit there. In a way, maybe it was good for her. She had a little audience there.

And I remember they were very nice people and we were all just so distraught over Millie, because something happened to her and I think she died. I'm not sure. She either died or went away, because she was no longer there and I was really sad when that happened. It may have happened before we moved to 14th Street. I must have been about eleven or twelve. I met some really nice people there, too. I was very taken with the man and woman who lived in the house next door. Phil Montagne had great charisma. He was always so friendly and she was very dignified, very beautiful. I was just taken with him. He was so nice. I asked him to be my godfather when I was confirmed. I think he was kind of surprised. Godparents usually gave boys watches. I wanted a watch for my confirmation present, but I got a Parker Pen set. I don't know where it is now, but I remember being very disappointed. I probably showed it, too. But he was always very kind. One time, we weren't going to have a turkey for Thanksgiving because we couldn't afford to buy one, and he rigged a raffle so that I would win the turkey!

My grandfather Di Pasquale loved music. He was the first farmer out there in the country to have a Victrola, and the first to have a radio. He didn't live long enough for TV. But if he did, he would have had that, too. He was always there, right there, in getting those new things. So because we were the ones with the Victrola, the parties were always held at his farmhouse there in the country. And there were musicians in the area who knew that my grandfather made great wine from his own grapes. And there is really nothing like that, if you like wine.

So, two or three times during the summer, we would

be asleep and all of a sudden we'd hear music outside in the driveway, at one or two in the morning. We'd wake up to guitars, mandolins, playing in the dark. The musicians had gotten out of their gigs and come by. They knew my grandfather would open the house to them. He'd get the homemade wine out and the food, and he just loved it. He'd roll back the rugs and we'd have a huge party.

How wonderful, how exciting it was, because he would have me sing with the musicians. I think I was about seven the first time I sang, maybe younger. They played mostly Italian music. My step-grandmother played the mandolin and sometimes she sang, too, but I always sang.

They would often have cocktail hour for some of the neighbors, who were mostly Swedish and loved to drink, and they knew about his wine. My grandfather would make people understand what he was saying, in his own kind of language, God knows what it was. And they would come by for a drink after work. It was quite a bistro we had going there. And I would sing then, too. In those days, you could buy song sheets, as they were called, with the lyrics. I kept up with all the current songs.

I got the biggest charge out of it because they all had this marvelous time. It was our own little United Nations, but with music and without the translators.

I loved the singing, I loved the music. That was born in me. My grandfather and my step-grandmother and their friends created a stage for me. I liked the attention they gave me, the attention and the sound of the music. I liked just the doing of it. I was so happy when I did it. It released me. So many people, when they sing, are not happy. That shocks me. I don't understand that. Are they afraid to show they're happy?

Step-grandmother Caterina had a brother and two

sisters and, either by some strange coincidence or maybe it was diabetes, they had each lost a leg. It was odd. Very weird. My step-grandmother was the only one in her family with both legs. My sisters and I still talk about it, to this day. At the farm, everyone would have a siesta in the afternoon. They would all come to the farm and where all these people slept, I will never know. We were always on the floor someplace. One day, we came running up the stairs—remember, we were children—and there, lined up along the railing were three false legs. We saw these three legs standing there with shoes on but no bodies, and we ran screaming down the stairs. It was scary, like a horror movie. Now we laugh about it. It was hysterical, bizarre and tragic, but it was so funny.

Caterina's sisters adored my mother. They were in her corner all the way. Caterina had a son from a previous marriage, and my father had my mother. I don't remember when this happened, but there was some kind of scheme that had to do with the farm. My parents and Caterina's son, Charles, and his wife, Lena, were supposed to put money into helping my grandparents, or helping the farm, something like a mortgage, maybe. My parents told Caterina's two sisters about it, because my mother was disturbed by the idea and I remember going to their house. Now, you would think they would be all for their own sister's son, but they said, "Don't you do it because your money would show up but we don't know that their money would show up." Uncle Charlie and Aunt Lena were the ones with the money. We had hardly any. I will never forget that. We might not have had the farm if it weren't for those two women. They were so smart. My step-grandmother may have been smart, too, but she may have been taken in by her son. She wasn't as sophisticated, if that's the word, as her sisters, who lived in the city and had city smarts. She had always lived in the country. But I will never forget their advice. My mother and father did not sign the papers. Their money might have gone pfft! We might have lost my grandfather's farm.

I led a very different life in Buffalo, in the winter. If the snow got to a certain depth, I don't remember how many feet, we had no school. And I loved not having school. Not that I didn't love school, I did, but it was like a special little gift holiday when you don't have to go anywhere outside the house and it was so quiet and it looked so pretty. We were never out of school for very long at all, even with all the snow. In Buffalo, it was just another fact of life.

In our next home, on Plymouth Avenue, I had my own room in the back, and it held a kind of large bed, a very wonderful desk, and there was a window that looked out into the neighbor's beautiful yard. That's all there was, but it was enough for my needs then. That's where I did all my studying.

I was very friendly with the lady next door, Mrs. D'Agostino. She had a huge Italian family with nine children. Every one of them was musical. Three of the boys played piano, and they were good. They were just a wonderful family. I was crazy about them. I got very close to them, especially two of the daughters, Angel and Cora. They were much older than I was, and Angel was married and becoming well-to-do. She was stunning. She would arrive there in the best car ever on the block. I just thought she was *it*. I became friendly with her and her husband. They had one child, a son. I've kept that friendship to this day.

Mrs. D'Agostino was like Anna Magnani, volatile and passionate. She had a dream that one of her children would make it in show business. She was very aggressive, but every one of her children disappointed her. They became musicians. They played in bands and taught music. They never wanted the big time and I did. It was really strange. The youngest child was a girl and she was a dancer. Mrs. D'Agostino wanted her to be the next Eleanor Powell. She went to dance class with a boy everyone was raving about, who grew up to be Michael Bennett, the famous choreographer of *Chorus Line* and all those big shows. He was from that little school in Buffalo.

Mrs. D'Agostino did take her youngest daughter to Hollywood. She took her everywhere, but the girl had no ambition. She had a boyfriend who never would let her go. They were together from the time they were in high school and they're still together. That's what she wanted. She did dance with Eleanor Powell's troupe, but that's the closest she got to fame. Then she quit. Her mother was fit to be tied.

So then Mrs. D'Agostino put all her energy and enthusiasm and interest into me. She came to every performance I ever did. She was a step-stage mother to me. The only one I ever had and the first one I ever met. To this day, I still see them. I sang at some of their weddings and Angel and her husband owned a town, outside of Buffalo. They were into all kinds of things. First they had a nightclub, the Tropicana, then they had a fabulous restaurant called The Cloisters. It was the most beautiful restaurant I have ever seen, with lovely art objects, and so tastefully done. Angel always looked great and was always up, just like her mother. I liked her husband, too. He was great. A long time later, Angel and her sister, Cora, came to New York. They just wanted me to escort them everywhere. I was rather poor then, probably between shows or club dates, so they filled my pockets with money and said, "Let's spend it!" We went to the Waldorf. We went to shows. We had the time of our lives. They were such great people. They had a love of life. Angel's a widow now, and a little subdued. It's hard for me to get used to that. But she had a street in their town named after her, and there's a covered bridge in that place named after her, too.

Mrs. D'Agostino lived to see Angel prosperous. She was very proud of her daughter. I had lunch with Angel in Buffalo a couple of years ago. She wanted me to see all of this. And I said, "None of this surprises me at all. This is the way it should be for you." It was wonderful having them next door. I sang with the sons who played piano, at parties we were always invited to. They were so good to us. It couldn't have been better than to have people like that next door.

On the other side lived a mother, a grandmother, and a son. He was my age and we went to high school together, but I had never met anyone like him before. He was, I guess, effete. He was blond, probably very gay, but I didn't know anything about that. He was different from everyone else I knew. He was bright, intelligent. He had a rough time in school, so of course I befriended him because I felt so bad for him. People just weren't nice. It was bad enough then, but it wasn't as bad as it could have been. His name was Charles. He wrote poetry. He was not a person you could get close to. He was like an Oscar Wilde character, lively, charming, interesting. They're fascinating but you never really get hold of them. That's the way he was.

It was an interesting kind of growing-up period, with him on one side and the D'Agostinos on the other, extremes of opposites.

In our house, the living room had an upright piano. I

had to practice at it while the boys on the block waited outside for me to come and play football. I must have been good at it, because they always waited for me. My mother saw to it that I practiced. The living room had very nice furniture, pretty lamps and a mirror. But for me, the prize was the bust of Schiller that had been a gift from friends in the country. Mr. and Mrs. George Wells lived down the road from Grandfather DiPasquale's farm. They were caretakers for a rich family and they lived in a little house across the road from the estate. They were a lovely couple, but lonely, and they had no life, no car, no nothing. At that time you couldn't go anywhere if you didn't drive. Mr. Wells had been given a bust of Schiller by his employers. I would go there and I would always say, "Oh, what I wouldn't give to have that statue, that bust of Schiller." I had such a response to it. It was so important to me at that age to have this kind of art close to me, so every time I went there, I would rave about the bust. One day, when I was about to graduate from high school, Mr. Wells said, "We want you to have the bust." I said, "Oh, wow, thank you, thank you!"

So the bust ended up sitting on our piano in the living room in Buffalo. It was the first art object I ever owned and now it's in my apartment in New York. I was sure I was going to drop it. It has a few chips here and there but it's still in great form and it has found its place with all my other art objects. I have some beautiful things but that bust was the beginning of my collection.

We had a handsome dining room. My mother just loved her dining set. We used it quite a lot for special occasions and holidays. All the rooms were quite large. There was a fireplace, but we never used it. There was a wonderful arch between the dining room and the living room. It made them look so elegant. There was a porch in the front and there was a backyard with rose bushes that I always had to cut.

So, it wasn't poor, it wasn't rich. It was sort of in between. Maybe the rent was thirty-five dollars a month, a lot in those days. The thing is, we always had a good house, a good home for people. To me it was really beautiful. After fifty years, we had to move my mother from that house because the landlord wanted it for his son who was getting married. It made us all very sad.

I have had so much kindness in my life. I'm just amazed, really. It's extraordinary. Maybe it was my reward for having to go to the landlady about being late with the rent: the bust of Schiller, the turkey and Mrs. D'Agostino, my first fan.

I used to have to go way over to another part of town for my piano lessons. I took three buses to get there and I remember the cold. It would really get cold. But I did it because I wanted to. I really loved those piano lessons. And it meant going into another stratum of living, to my Aunt Lena, who had paintings and two pianos. It was just a different world and very often I'd stay there for dinner. That was where I had Chinese food for the first time. I must have been twelve when I first started going to her house. When she first taught me, she lived much nearer to our neighborhood and she came to me, so it was easy.

One of the great things about living in Buffalo was that people there really supported my talent and my singing, because from the time that I can remember, that's what I wanted to do. From my childhood, they were always there, urging me to sing, urging me to perform, taking me places. They were in my corner, which was really lucky. All the friends and relatives: they were just there.

In those days, when I was really young, they had

what they called amateur nights, all over the place. I went to every amateur contest that you could name, and, invariably, I would win. I would win something like twenty-five dollars, quite a lot of money during the Depression, a month's rent.

So it was wonderful and to me it was fun. I just had a good time. It was such a good time that I never realized that you had to put a money value on singing, so it took me a while to know how to do that. Singing was just such a natural function for me that I found putting a price tag on it difficult. Later, fortunately, I had other people to do that. I couldn't think of it that way.

My parents would take me to these small neighborhood clubs that were all over the place in those days. We had movies and radio, but no television then. So there were all these wonderful little clubs to go to and they all had shows. I don't know how good the talent was, but they all had singers and comics and dancers. People would go on Friday or Saturday nights. That was their only entertainment. So I would get dressed up and my parents would take me and I would sing and I would make some money. The audience would throw money at me, mostly coins, and I had to pick it up. That was painfully embarrassing for me. Sometimes, when I went around to the tables, they would give me dollar bills. We lived on that money.

But I just loved performing! I didn't really think about the money or even the attention. That I was getting a lot of attention wasn't really it. It was just the joy of singing. I just loved doing it. Right from those days, I had support. The teachers in the schools all recognized my talent and I was used in all the school performances. I was always the announcer, I sang and acted in all the plays. When I went to high school, after my voice changed, the music teacher, Mr. Pelletier, said, "You have got to study music." I didn't know where to go, and he told me there was a school in Buffalo, the First Settlement Music School (now the Community Music School) that had wonderful teachers, but you didn't have to pay very much because it was backed by the wealthy of the city and they supported it. So that's where I went. When I told my parents about the First Settlement Music School, my father said we just didn't have the money to pay the two dollars each lesson cost. I'd have to work for the money. Luckily, a neighbor had a route delivering magazines and out-of-town newspapers and needed a helper. The job meant getting up at about five A.M. and working for three hours a week, at seventy-five cents an hour. I took the job and developed an incurable need for the *New York Times*. It's my drug of choice and satisfies my curiosity about the past, present and future of an ever-changing world. I doubt I'll ever shake that addiction.

And I was very fortunate then, too, because there were several teachers and I wanted the teacher who taught Norma Coffas, a girl I was kind of infatuated with, who was singing on radio at a very young age. She had a lovely coloratura soprano voice. When I went to speak to the Director of the school, she assigned me to another teacher, Louise E. Sleep. At first I wasn't too happy about it, but it turned out to be the luckiest thing that ever happened because it was Mrs. Sleep's teacher that I finally went to study with, the great William L. Whitney, at the New England Conservatory of Music in Boston.

I don't know where I would have gone, really. I don't think I would have had *bel canto* training, either. So I was happy, very happy with her, after I got over the initial disappointment.

The First Settlement Music School was on the west

side of Buffalo, where we lived, but it was quite a walk. It was a good walk. I liked it. I walked through a lot of weather to get to it, absolutely, but somehow I got used to it. When you're young, the weather doesn't seem to matter so much.

Voice students had to take chorus at the School. We used to go from six to eight, or seven to nine, in the evening. It was dark and very cold. It was a small school. I was about sixteen when, one night, there was a disturbance at the door. There were adults in this chorus, a mix of adults, teenagers and young kids. The teacher was the lady who ran the school, Dorothy Hebb. She was very strong. I liked her. I had never met anyone quite like her. She seemed to me as much male as female, which made her very powerful. She was tall and she was strong and she could run a school. She had that authority about her.

So there we were in chorus, singing, one night and someone kept pounding on the door. It was scary. Mrs. Hebb didn't know how to handle it. It had never happened before. The school was on a very good street, with large homes, sort of affluent, so you didn't expect that kind of thing to happen and everyone was scared. It kept up and kept up and kept up. Finally she said, "Andy, would you go and take care of that?"

I didn't know any better because I was young, but when I look back at it, I think it was amazing that of all these people, she would tell me to go and deal with it. I guess she knew that whatever this way was that I had of dealing with people, I could manage. So I went out and a man, disheveled and quite drunk, was in the vestibule between the inside door and the storm door. I went out to him and told him what was happening, what we were doing, and that we couldn't sing and we couldn't make music if he was going to keep on making noise, and we

26

would appreciate his leaving and wished there was something we could do for him but we were all very poor people and we were just here, trying to get out of our own misery. And he went away.

When I was about seventeen, I started visualizing a career. I didn't realize that visualizing was a power, a very strong power. I could see myself performing on radio, which was quite the thing then. I was taking my singing lessons and visualizing myself performing on the radio and one day, after a singing lesson, I made a wrong turn. I was in such a state, the way you are after a singing lesson, very high on oxygen and happiness, that I wasn't thinking and I ended up in front of a radio station, WEBR, and I thought, there must be a reason for this. I didn't stop to think about it. I just walked in and said, "I want to see the program director." The secretary said, "Well, there he is, he's going up the stairs." So I just followed him up the stairs and I said, "I would like to audition for you. I'm a singer." He said, "Well, how about right now?" I said, "That would be great. I've got my music."

So he took me into a studio and called in a pianist and I sang and the scene was right out of a movie. He said, "Well, I really love your voice and I'd like to try you on a show." He put me on a show on January 18, 1942, my eighteenth birthday. What a birthday present! I did really well. I remember I sang a Jerome Kern song, "More and More," that was written for a Deanna Durbin movie.

Afterward, he called me into his office and said, "I'm putting together a new show and I want you on it. You will sing with a full orchestra, twenty musicians, and it's going to be geared to the armed forces. It's called "Armed Forces Mail Call." You will read letters sent by servicemen asking for songs to be sung to their wives or sweethearts, and vice versa."

I was thrilled to death with this because I had started college and I needed the money desperately. I had gotten a scholarship to Canisius College, a wonderful Jesuit school, and even though my sights were set on Mr. Whitney at the New England Conservatory of Music, I knew that I had to accept the scholarship at Canisius. It would have been foolish not to do it, so I put that dream off for a couple of years. I needed more training anyway. I accepted the scholarship and became the soloist for the Glee Club. That was the reason for the scholarship. It was a very big thing in those days, that Glee Club. It was all male voices and it was a beautiful group.

So I was going to college and doing "Armed Forces Mail Call" every morning at nine o'clock, five days a week. It was like a Regis Philbin and Kathy Lee show, without Kathy Lee. The orchestra was made up of the best musicians in Buffalo. They were terrific and it was a one-hour show. I did a lot of songs every day. I would have to get up at six-thirty and vocalize and then my wonderful father would drive me to the station so I could be there at eight. Then, at ten, I'd go to school. It was really astonishing how that all worked out! I did that show for two and a half years, until the war was over. It was an amazing thing. Actually, that's as long as the college pre-law course lasted. It was an accelerated program and it went on for two and a half years instead of four. My parents wanted me to study something they felt was a little more secure than show business, so I decided to take pre-law, of all things, knowing that I would never use it. Of course, it did give me credits that I used when I went to Boston!

In 1944, Dorothy Hebb, the head of the First Settlement Music School, said, "You know you must take music theory and sight singing. You'll need both when you go to Boston." The School arranged for me to study with

Charles Nichols and Squire Haskin, and paid for it. They were musicians. Charles Nichols was an organist and Squire Haskin was a pianist with the Buffalo Symphony. They were very intellectual, very skilled musicians. I learned a lot about theory and sight-singing from them. I kept my friendship with them going after I went to Boston. I would write to them occasionally and tell them about my progress. I would try to see them when I went home. Charles Nichols eventually moved to Boston to take an important teaching position and play at a big church there. I did see him several times, but then he died. I would see Squire Haskin in Buffalo at Christmas vacations and bring him a little gift. He had this wonderful small house in an area that's like the Greenwich Village of Buffalo, like Chelsea. There was a whole musical group there that revolved around the First Settlement Music School, all very talented people, professional voice teachers, pianists, instrumentalists. I was too young to grasp how good they really were and how committed they were. Then, in the late 1980s, someone entered Squire Haskin's house and killed him. It was horrible. I couldn't believe it. I hadn't seen him in a long time. Even so, I was devastated. It was so uncalled for. He was such a gentleman. That's the word for him: gentleman.

In 1945, the Buffalo Foundation helped young artists from the surrounding area with their educations. Of course, I had built up quite a reputation. Everybody knew me because of that radio program. I got a lot of other work from it, too, other jobs, club dates and things around town. Because of that, the Foundation became interested and gave me a thousand dollars for my first year at the New England Conservatory of Music and they raised it every year while I was in Boston. I came back while I was at the Conservatory and did a benefit for them and another one for the First Settlement Music School where I got my early training.

I'll never forget it. I wrote a letter not long ago to the Buffalo Foundation, saying what had happened to me since, and how much their help meant to me and that I just wanted them to know that. I got a wonderful letter back and they were very appreciative. I suppose they do keep a record of the scholarships and gifts to artists.

I took advantage of everything I could. I don't know where that came from. My parents were not like that at all, not at all. I just took advantage of every opportunity. I was aggressive. My mother was, to a certain extent, but not my father. I took advantage of every situation and I just wouldn't let things get by. I had the courage or the *chutzpah,* or whatever it is, to follow it, and never thought that it was too much or I was too aggressive or too this or too that. I just did it, whether my parents approved of it or not. I never had those kinds of judgments about anything. Most of the time it worked out really well. So that's how I got to Boston, with the help of my parents, the First Settlement Music School, Charles Nichols and Squire Haskin, the Buffalo Foundation and the Conservatory itself.

I couldn't wait to get to Boston to study with William L. Whitney at the New England Conservatory of Music. Mrs. Sleep had psyched me up for him so much, she just couldn't wait, either. It had been her dream that one of her students would go to study with him. This woman had taught voice in Buffalo for thirty years but not one person had done it. And she had some talented singers. I always felt that I was the one who was going to do it. I had to do it, for myself and for her. When I did, she was thrilled and so was I.

III

Boston

Leaving Buffalo for Boston should have been a snap for me. I had a history of paid and unpaid performances, starting when I was five years old, in schools, theaters, cafés, clubs, on radio, in front of every kind of audience, with every level of accompaniment, right through to a full symphony orchestra. As a child, I had gotten work on the "Children's Hour," a radio show in Buffalo that used young, talented children. From that, I got invitations to perform for fraternal organizations. My father drove me to all these places. Tired as he might be, it always made him happy. One special time, after I got my B.A. from the Conservatory, I sang with the Buffalo Philharmonic at Kleinhans Music Hall. How happy, how thrilled he was when he came backstage. I was used to my mother's approval, but my father never told me how he felt about my performances before. I guess he didn't want to "spoil" me or "give me a big head," an unforgivable pair of sins in those days.

I can see that dressing room, my father is with me. How happy he was that I was doing this fantastic program. It was another new world to him. I was the soloist with the most important orchestra in Buffalo and a chorus of a hundred voices. I opened with a wonderful arrangement of "Begin the Beguine." He was so moved by my performance, by the audience's reception of me. He couldn't say the words even then, but his face and manner told me he was a proud father and a happy man.

Singing was such a natural thing for me. I didn't ever feel what people describe as "stage fright" or "performance anxiety." I didn't sing for the applause or the reviews. Singing was what I loved to do, had always done and still love to do. Singing and the teaching of singing have been my life.

To the uninitiated, going to the New England Conservatory of Music with a partial scholarship for four years could have seemed almost unnecessary. Not to my parents. Some people have "stage" mothers and fathers; I had "college" parents.

I'd need continued help from my whole family and every job I could get. My private lessons with Mr. Whitney were horribly expensive and absolutely necessary. In 1943, my mother had gone to work, first at Berger's, then at Morrison's department stores. My sisters took on the housekeeping and cooking. My father worked seven days a week at his business, Al's Upholstery. Mother worked from October through June, then when school closed she and the girls went to the farm to help Grandfather Giacomo. Step-grandmother Caterina died in 1942, maybe from complications of diabetes. Mother did the housework and we all did farm work, and picked the crops. She canned and preserved vegetables and fruits for the whole family.

I am still overwhelmed by their demonstration of love for and belief in me. Now I was twenty-one. It was 1945. The war was over. I was not alone in my struggle. I was so lucky!

How did they do it? Six more years of hard work and self-denial, and they never complained, never referred to their generosity to me, ever. They all believed in my tal-

32

ent and my own commitment to a Master's Degree in Music and a career in show business. They knew I had absolute concentration on my visualized goal, that I would not waste their hard work or mine, or their faith in me.

My musical education and the career I sought was our family goal. I had a small but effective army behind me. Without them, I might have made it, but it would have been so much harder. No words exist to describe my lifelong gratitude to my family.

I went to Boston by train, carrying my music, some clothes and the knowledge that Boston would be my home for the next six years. I'd see my family on vacations. I was on my own for the first time in my life. I was accountable to no one but myself. I got off the train with a hundred dollars in my pocket, to live on until I got a job. My parents helped me, but if I wanted or needed anything except the basic necessities, I'd have to earn it myself. I could visualize what I wanted my life in Boston to be like, but I had to work for it. Everything would be new, and I was eager to get to the Conservatory, register, get my dorm assignment, drop off my stuff and go look for a job. I was hungry so after registration, I went to the YMCA coffee shop next door for something to eat, and then and there I got my first job helping the baker, and met the most important person I would ever meet in Boston, except for Mr. Whitney and a young man named Johnny King. This person was a hard-of-hearing waitress who knew someone who knew Mrs. Margaret Richards, the wife of Dr. Theodore Richards, a Nobelist in chemistry.

I went to my dorm room in a brownstone not far from the Conservatory and met fellow students. Then it was time to prepare for my first day at the bakery, where I had to be at five A.M. Classes started around ten, and I was scheduled for my first meeting with Mr. Whitney, too.

I remember meeting him like it was yesterday. He was a very beautiful man. Even at his age, he still had a glow. His face was hardly wrinkled. He changed my voice in that first lesson. Somehow, through the exercises, he got my voice totally covered. I didn't know all that then, but when I felt the cover, I knew what it was. That experience was unforgettable. He knew he'd done it and his interest in me just grew and grew. If a student gets it like that, then you know that they're going to do something big with it. Mr. Whitney was in his late eighties. Perhaps what happened to him then is happening to me now. It's the accumulation of knowledge, wisdom, action and age. It attracts people who want the benefits these things can offer. He never spoke much. He never described or spoke of what was actually going on. My voice changed strictly through the exercises. He did say, "Tip your chin and lift your chest." We talked about the breathing a little bit, but it was mostly done through the exercises. He never went into long discussions. It was that simple. Sometimes he didn't even say that, because he would make a motion and I knew what it meant. He would put the base of his palms against the front of the piano keyboard and cup his fingers into his palm. I associated that with lifting the chest and tipping my chin down, simultaneously lifting my palate, and so covering the voice. That day I knew I had done it. I knew I had experienced something tremendous because I walked into his room with one voice and walked out with another. I knew the feeling and could duplicate it from that time on. This was quite remarkable. It doesn't always work that way. I understood it and I couldn't wait to get back into that room. I was so eager to work with him and to get the training from him that I was totally open to the knowledge that he poured into me.

I wasn't in my own way at all.

Mrs. Sleep, in Buffalo, had prepared me very well but I didn't do with her what I did with Mr. Whitney. She kept my voice very healthy, very easy. Men's voices go through a definite change in the cover. When I walked out of his studio that first day, I was a totally different person. I knew I had hit on the truth and I was a happy man. The feeling I used to have going into his room was truly mystical, spiritual.

When I go back to the Conservatory now, I always go by that room and genuflect and thank God for Mr. Whitney, and for Mrs. Sleep, who never pushed my voice beyond its natural setting.

I worked every day at the YMCA coffee shop from half past five till ten, then during the lunch hour, so I had those two meals paid for by the sweat of my brow. The baker always had great sweet rolls ready when I got there, and I'd have them and go to work, then breakfast and I'd be off to school. I needed another job to pay for dinner, but hadn't found it yet. But they had these wonderful little eating places around the Conservatory. People opened up their homes and turned them into tea rooms or small garden restaurants. It was home cooking. They were very cheap. There's nothing like them around today. You can't just cook a meal and serve it to the public. But I still needed that other job. One hundred dollars didn't mean I could survive for a whole semester.

A couple of months later, my dear parents drove to Boston to see me. My uncle Tony shared the drive. Nowadays it's a round trip of about nine hundred miles on I-90, but in 1945, with the war just over, it was a long, slow journey on badly maintained two-lane roads, through a hundred towns with their stop signs, red lights, potholes and school buses, on old, worn-out tires. They had accepted my overwhelming desire to spend my life in music. They helped me to reach my goal from then on. They came to reassure themselves that I was eating properly, living in a decent neighborhood. Mom took a picture of Dad and me, standing a little distance apart, in front of his car. They didn't stay long but it meant the world to me. I was on my path but I surely missed my family. Mom wouldn't leave until I agreed to send my laundry home for her to do. In those days, again, it was cheaper to mail stuff back and forth than to take it to a laundry, and she estimated it would save me about ten dollars a month. There were no laundromats yet. It was 1945 and so many things we take for granted now just didn't exist.

Mr. Whitney took such an interest in me from the beginning and boy, he threw me into some very difficult music right off the bat. Huge ranges. He put me in a program at the Conservatory right away. For the first time in my life, I got nervous about singing. I wasn't quite ready, or so I thought. So I called the school and said I had a cold and couldn't do the program. I didn't go to school that day. I was living at the top of a three-story brownstone and at two o'clock, the doorbell rang. My room mate answered and said to me, "You're not going to believe this. Mr. Whitney is on his way up." I think I had a healing right there, right then. *If he gets up here,* I thought, *he'll die and it'll be my fault!* He sat down and talked, then he said, "How are you feeling?"

I really wasn't sure how I was feeling.

He said, "Do you have any voice at all?"

I said, "I think I do."

He said, "Would you be willing to give it a go? I will play for you."

That was quite an honor because he didn't play for everybody.

I said, "Well, that's an offer I can't resist."

So I did sing and my cold was psychosomatic and there was nothing wrong with my voice and he knew it. He knew I was just nervous. I had to do two pieces from Haydn's "The Seasons" and they're very difficult and I was afraid of them because they went up to high E's and down to low G's and they had all these runs in them. Mr. Whitney was allergic to ivory so he always had to wear white cotton gloves when he played. They were the talk of the school, those white gloves. So to relax me, he didn't put on the gloves till he sat down at the piano. It felt to me like it took twenty minutes for him to put them on, slowly, and the audience laughed and I laughed. I did my first Conservatory performance and it was fine.

I can still feel the energy I felt when I used to walk into his room. There was a feeling there, a sensation, that I've never felt since. I knew I was in the presence of greatness and I knew it was going to change my life.

Mr. Whitney died when he was ninety-three. I was still at the Conservatory and I missed him dreadfully. But I had him for almost four years. I was very fortunate. It seemed that he had lasted, held on, just for me, so I could learn his technique and pass it on. I really believe that. One day, he went from the piano, from giving a lesson, to the ambulance, to the hospital, and almost immediately died. I thought that was so wonderful. What a way to go! He never suffered. I was told he was joking with the attendants in the ambulance.

The essence of that man has stayed with me all my life.

Classes at the Conservatory included languages: French, German and Italian. My Italian professor must have been from Florence, Italy, because when I would, absentmindedly, drop in a Sicilian word or phrase, he would literally shriek, *"Italiano!"* and the class would find it very funny. I guess it broke up the monotony. Then there was music theory, harmony, or sight-singing, opera classes, coaching classes, chorus and voice lessons in addition to my private sessions with Mr. Whitney. I didn't study piano. My Aunt Lena's teaching was so good, I was able to teach myself transposing! I also studied dance and stage movement privately at the then smaller Boston Conservatory of Dance, with Jan Veen.

The biggest personal surprise happened to me on a Saturday afternoon, after I had done the weekly recital program all the voice students had to do. It was my second recital and at the end I came back stage and there was the most elegant, dignified dowager standing there. She was a stunning woman. She must have been about eighty years old. She said, "I have to speak with you. My name is Margaret Richards and I have to follow your career, because you have IT. I've told that to only one other performer in my life, and I've never said it since that time."

I asked her, "Who was that?" hoping she'd say Caruso.

She said, "I went to a play with a new actress in it and that girl had IT. Her name was Ingrid Bergman."

I said, "Oh thank you so much."

She said, "I play the piano very well. Would you like to come to my hotel in Cambridge and go over some music? And then we can have dinner."

Dinner?

"Oh, yes, wow!"

Her apartment was gorgeous, the dinner was fabulous, and she told me of her Nobel prize-winning-chemist husband, Theodore Richards. Her daughter was married to James F. Conant, President of Harvard. And Margaret

Richards was a virtuoso accompanist.

Mrs. Richards brought me into a whole world that I knew existed but had never been a part of. I learned so much from this wonderful lady. Every Saturday she went over my music with me for hours, for four whole years. She came to every performance I did. We were the talk of the Conservatory. She would always show up for my performances and we would go to the Parker House, right in Boston proper. Through her I met the Conants. I met all the literati. I sang and did programs there. It was just an unbelievable opening up for me. It brought me into the world I wanted to be a part of. I learned all about manners and courtesy, real dignity, real beauty. She played so well. It seemed to give her such joy and it gave me great joy too because I was learning my music and she loved teaching me. And I had the best meal of the week! I used to look forward to Saturdays so much. I was so far from home and she took me into her life. I had found a second mother. Now I went to football games, parties, everything. I was part of Harvard without being a student there. Because of her interest in me, they took me into their homes. She came to my graduation and is on film with my dear mother and father. She was one of the most important people in my life.

Whenever I went home, I always kept in touch with her, and after I left Boston for New York, I kept writing to her. I even got her to come to Chatauqua one summer and she had a wonderful time there. Years later, I went to see her, and she opened the door, looking just as regal as when I first saw her. She looked like royalty and she was what royalty ought to be and often isn't. But this time she didn't know me. I was heartbroken that she had forgotten me, lost all those wonderful memories. I'm afraid it was Alzheimer's. She died not too long after that.

All those years she took me to concerts, to the symphony, all things I couldn't pay for. She was totally supportive of me. She always gave me compliments on my work, on changes she noticed in my voice and performance. She loved me as much as my family did, and I loved her wholeheartedly. I miss her still, and when I'm in Boston, I see her everywhere we used to go.

I often think of the fact that if I hadn't gotten the job at the YMCA coffee shop and helped out the waitress who was partially deaf, who gave my name to someone who knew Mrs. Richards, and told her where to find me, I would never have experienced that whole life-changing metamorphosis.

The Conservatory had a bulletin board and calls for student performers were posted on it. That was where I found my first paid singing job, at an Episcopal church in Wellesley, outside of Boston. So I called them and auditioned and these people just took me in. They were wonderful to me. They loved the way I sang. Of course, they weren't paying me that much, so I was invited to their homes on Sundays for dinner, right after church. I used to take a bus to Wellesley for rehearsals, but on Sundays the organist and his wife, who lived in Boston, would drive me out.

There was one family I really got close to, the Pikes. Mrs. Pike had been a singer and she was a dynamo. Mr. Pike was the sweetest man but he really couldn't hold that woman down. She had a daughter, Vita, and a son. Vita was a terrific girl, so alive, so open, so charming.

I'd been in Boston for a year and I was starting to look for more opportunities to sing in new places. Mrs. Pike got me community theater work. I just can't forget one of the shows I did there. I sang, "I've Got You Under My Skin." Well, the house came down. I had never received applause like that. Wow!

I'd stay overnight at the Pikes' house after the buses stopped running. Mrs. Pike was a smart woman and she knew I was on the right track with my voice. She'd say, "Don't listen to anyone. You are doing it right. Stay with it. Don't get distracted." I needed to hear that. It was rough because I still didn't have any money. How could I take a girl out, without money? Vita understood that. I had a job at a record shop downtown in Boston that year. Vita would meet me after work and then we'd go out and have dinner. We went Dutch. A lot of the time she'd pick up the tab. I couldn't.

I was never in my room. I just went there to sleep. I had a nice room mate, Donald Emerson. There were two boys across the hall who were at the Conservatory, too. It was the least interesting of all the places I lived in, kind of seedy, with strange people running in and out. A typical student boarding house.

A big treat was going to Howard Johnson's on Sundays for chicken croquettes. I loved their chicken croquettes. Everyone else loved their hot dogs and malteds but chicken croquettes were a new experience for me.

All my life I've had people helping me and giving to me. I wasn't working at it, or trying to get something. I was guileless, naïve. I didn't have any street smarts. I was happy then. It was all ahead of me. I always knew where I was going: to New York, to Broadway, and I wasn't going to let anything get in my way. A girl friend, a wife, children? There was no way I'd get to my goal down that road. Educating, feeding and housing myself took every ounce of strength I could muster. I had to learn a lot about how to take care of myself. But I did, and with the help of Margaret Richards and the Pikes, I was exposed to a different world. I had never known that life held such vast differences of race and social class. Wellesley was very white-bread and WASPy. Here I was, this young, this very young, second generation Sicilian-American. All I had to do was open my mouth and sing and that was it. They accepted me. The Pikes were very musical. They went to the symphony, theater, opera. They had the money to do all those things. They recognized my potential, so that was, I am sure, the reason for their interest in me.

All those things were part of the mosaic of the Conservatory, Mrs. Richards and the community theater of Wellesley, that widened my horizons. I was very enterprising and I did what I had to do to stay there.

My family wanted me home on Christmas Eve, but I stayed to do the Christmas service in Wellesley. That and Easter were the two most important church rites, so I had to be there. My family was wonderful about it. They never carried on or made a fuss. They knew I'd finally get home somehow.

On Christmas Eve in Boston, there was always something happening. I wanted to experience Christmas Eve on Beacon Hill. The Conservatory students would get together and go caroling, and the Hill families would invite us into these marvelous old houses and they'd feed us. Then I'd rush off to Wellesley and sing, rush back to Boston and get a train to Buffalo, usually arriving just in time for breakfast and Mass at our church. I still manage to celebrate Christmas in at least two different places.

Another way to hear great music if you were a student was to usher at Symphony Hall. They didn't pay you but you could hear the concert. They gave you a locker and you put your coat in it, they handed you a jacket and a pile of programs, and heaven.

In my second year, I had to change my routine. I

moved to a room in an apartment on Bay State Road, off the Charles River, in a beautiful brownstone. I used the practice rooms at the Conservatory late into the evenings, so getting up at five A.M. was an impossibility. I needed a different job, so I visualized something musical, near where I was living, that would give me flexible hours. And there it was, a big building that said, "The Boston Music Company," right near my new room. I went in, asked for the manager, said I was a second-year student at the Conservatory and that I would like very much to work there. He hired me on the spot. I was there every afternoon during my breaks, three or four hours. I unpacked the new music that came in and put it up on the right shelves. When they got orders, the staff would go directly to the shelves and send the music out. A wonderful group of people worked there, very kind, very helpful. I could work whenever my hours permitted. But I still wanted to find a way to make money through my singing. I didn't want to do just anything. I had started singing at clubs in Boston on Friday and Saturday nights. There were quite a few then. I didn't care what they were like. I knew I couldn't start off at the Copley Plaza. I knew I had to come up with an act for the clubs that was unique.

There was a girl, Emmalina DeVita, with a magnificent voice. I first saw her and heard her sing at the Conservatory when she was fifteen or sixteen. She wasn't a student then. I just happened to go in and hear her on a program. I thought she was talented, so I waited till she was finished and went back and told her how talented I thought she was, and how I couldn't wait for her to come to the Conservatory. By the time she did, I had met a young man named Dana Lordly. I had never seen anybody so handsome in my life. I found out that he was a student, a pianist from Saskatchewan in Canada. We became friends. He played piano magnificently and would play all my music for me. He wouldn't take money from me. Dana and I came up with the idea for a specialty act, when he met Emmalina and fell in love with her voice. He loved people with real talent, especially singers. He was a fine accompanist. He couldn't sing but he loved playing for singers. The act was called "Musical Portraits." We opened as a still life. This was my idea. I thought it would be great to start it as a portrait and then bring it to life as the music started, and we became real. We did opera scenes. We acted them out and did duets and solos. Then Dana would play something of Rachmaninoff's, or Tchaikovsky's. He was very good at that romantic repertoire and it suited him. He made great arrangements. Sometimes we'd do medleys from operettas, or Broadway shows.

We auditioned for a big concert agent in Boston, a woman named Margaret Richardson. (Was it fate or coincidence?) She took us under her wing and fell in love with Dana. He had charm. I was the naïve one, but I knew what an asset that was. Men and women, children, cats, dogs, they all fell for him. Unbelievable! Dana handled the business end with Mrs. Richardson. We got fabulous jobs. It was a really high-class act. We did it for all kinds of audiences and they loved it.

After a couple of years, Mrs. Richardson sponsored us in a big concert at one of the important halls in Boston. That's how much she loved us. By that time, she was thinking of retiring. I'm not sure how it happened, if it was her idea or Dana's, but he must have wanted to get into the agency business. He kept it a secret from Emmalina and me. Dana had to come up with money to buy into the agency and he didn't have it. Mrs. Richardson found a man named Dane (again, fate or coincidence?) who had

the money. They joined forces. Dana never asked me if I
wanted to come in on the deal. He knew I wanted to get to
New York. Dana didn't want to go there. I said, "You're
making the biggest mistake of your life. You do not belong
here. You do not belong in a concert agency. You belong in
New York. With your talent and your looks, you would
take the town by storm. It would be a wonderful way for
all of us to come to New York, with this act."

But he really wanted something he believed would be
more secure. He decided to stay with the agency and it
was the beginning of the end. The name of the business
became "Lordly & Dane." It's still there, without him, a
speaker's agency. He started to drink when the pressures
of the business got too much for him. He wasn't really
geared for that. "Musical Portraits" went on without
Emmalina and me, after we left for New York. He continued the act but he didn't perform much outside of the act.
He started to make more money. He really built the business. The new money man just used him to build the business.

I was so shocked when I realized that Dana was
drinking. One night, we were sitting in the apartment
that belonged to his aunt. He was drinking and he started
to cry. He was on a crying jag. I knew about that because
I had an uncle who would get into them. I preached to
him that he had to do something about this, that it was
really bad, that he was slowly losing those fabulous looks.
Then I saw him in New York a few times and the same
thing happened. I just couldn't watch this man disinte-
grate. I cared about him. He could have been a star. He
had charisma. That's what I used to say to him. Even
then I had an eye for talent, but he was just too far gone.
Finally they had to let him go from the agency. I spoke to
the money man several times because I wanted to be sure

that they were doing something to take care of him. Dana never knew I did that. Then I heard he was conducting a chorus of singers in Canada.

Then my friend, Charlotte Shork, another student at the Conservatory, who was madly in love with Dana, called me to say he had committed suicide. I was devastated. I knew nothing about the power of an addiction then.

Charlotte was tall, willowy and beautiful. She had a fine voice but she never pursued a career. She married Freeman Higgins, from a long line of blue-bloods. He was a lot older than she was. She bought his whole mystique: ancestry, old money, good looks. Then Charlotte became an alcoholic and when Dana died, it got even worse. I just couldn't bear it, seeing her come apart, too.

Another fellow student, Carroll Saint, an actor and singer, was a very good friend of mine. He was a wonderful man. He got jobs and things were just beginning to break for him. He was in his middle thirties. He married Catherine, an actress in New York. Emmalina and I saw a lot of him. The marriage didn't work. They had a son. Catherine was pushing Carroll hard, but he wasn't making enough money. He must have been desperate because he took an overdose of sleeping pills. I couldn't believe it was deliberate.

He had a big insurance policy and his wife and child would be taken care of. Catherine couldn't face going to the morgue. She called a friend of mine, Johnny King, and asked him to go to the morgue and identify Carroll's body. I was on tour, and Johnny told me later it was awful. Carroll was just a slab of meat, lying on a metal shelf in a cold, bleak room.

It's sad that three of the people I was closest to in Boston drank and two of them committed suicide. I did not understand why they drank, why they didn't pursue their goals. I couldn't help them, though I tried.

Just about this time, when it seemed that all my visualized goals were being met, I stepped on that classic show business banana peel called "playing the game."

It happened (where else?) in Buffalo, my home town. I was the star of a benefit concert for my alma mater, now the Community Music School. Family, friends, fans and teachers attended, expecting they would have a great evening.

Well, they didn't get it. I was awful and I knew it. The faithful always applaud, no matter how bad you are. I took one bow and ran off stage, straight to the men's room, where I threw up. I skipped the reception. I couldn't bear it. I was sure my life in music was over.

How did it happen? Now I can tell the whole story. It's a cautionary tale for performers.

A new voice coach had arrived at the Conservatory. His name was Felix Wolfes and he was a voice coach for the Metropolitan Opera. Mr. Whitney got me a partial scholarship so I could study with this man. Mr. Wolfes brought in a new voice teacher, Mme. Ellsberg. She needed students and she was Mr. Wolfes's protégé. What better way to solidify my contact with Mr. Wolfes than to take some lessons from her?

So I did. The way she taught was totally opposite from Mr. Whitney's technique. She wanted a wide-open, pushing sound. I had never sung that way in my life but I tried to do it her way. Students do that with a new teacher.

I remember one lesson with Mme. Ellsberg. I was doing an aria and my voice slipped right into the cover. She said, "That was good." Stupidly, I replied, "That's what Mr. Whitney teaches me." She went right back to demanding I do it her way, fast.

I was always happy to do a benefit concert for my beloved Community Music School so when the request came in, I said I'd be there. The big night arrived and I opened my mouth and out came this dreadful, noisy, grating sound. The exercises and vocalization out of the cover had done their worst. I stuck it out but I was mortified. I was dreadful.

There was more horror to come. Theodolina Boris was Buffalo's music critic and she had heard me sing many times. She was always complimentary, always in my corner. Her review of this fiasco just devastated me. She wanted to know what had happened to my voice, and blamed Boston for the problem.

I didn't take another minute, much less an hour, with Mme. Ellsberg. I never told Mr. Whitney of the disaster. I studied with him until he died. And I never sang out of the cover again.

Like any good teacher, I use my life's triumphs and traumas to show my students that everyone can make a mistake, but not everyone can recognize it and learn from it. I was lucky. I had learned early that for a singer, performance must come before politics. If a teacher opens up your voice and you climb to new highs and lows, more richness, and you enjoy your classes, stick with that teacher. Don't go looking for contacts from a teacher, though it's great if he or she had them. Agents are for contacts. Teachers are for singing.

Over the six years in Boston, I stayed friendly with my house mates, but I was older and I wanted to live someplace nicer. After the first year, I lived mostly by myself. I had my own room one time, in somebody's large apartment where there were a number of bedrooms and everyone shared the kitchen and bath. But I wanted to live on Beacon Hill. In my fifth year, I found this wonder-ful little apartment there, and a Jewish landlady who was so good to me. She would come to hear me sing. It had a little kitchen and bath. My friend, Johnny King, helped me to wallpaper it. I was in my Chinese period then, so it was Chinese wallpaper. I thought it was charming. I left for New York from that apartment.

I had been rather lonely until I met Dana Lordly, and he and Emmalina and I did "Musical Portraits." Then I started my study for a master's degree. I was making enough money so that my family didn't have to send me money, but mother insisted I keep sending my laundry to her to do. She thought prices in Boston were a scandal and would have sent me cooked meals if she could.

That last year, I had my first students as part of the master's program. I wasn't really making money from them. I do regret that I didn't think of myself as a teacher, then. I would have liked to do more teaching. If I had told this to Mr. Whitney in the beginning, I could probably be at the Conservatory, teaching, today. But what I would have missed! So it all worked out the way it was supposed to, if there is a "supposed to." And I like the way it worked out. I think about these things and the good memories come back, along with the sad things I had to cope with, alone, for the first time in all my life.

I met another student, Rosalind Elias, who later became one of the youngest singers ever at the Metropol-itan Opera. I think she has had the longest-running career at the Met, too. She was a mezzo soprano and she and Emmalina were very close. Rosalind really concen-trated on her goal and succeeded.

When Emmalina decided to go to Europe to study, her craziness got in her way. She went to Germany and met Tullio Seraphin, the famous conductor who really put

Maria Callas on the top. Emmalina always imagined herself to be another Callas. She had that kind of voice, but hers had a prettier quality. She could do it all, everything that Callas did. She even did *Salome.* She could act and had the inner freedom to make it. Seraphin was wild about her. He knew he had found another great talent, but this was Germany and he didn't quite get her carrying on. He was from the old school and he may have thought that she was frivolous or that she wasn't committed, but she was. Her manner was just not professional. It all ended badly. I think she became a nurse in Germany, then she came back home to live with her mother.

Rosalind Elias kept up with her. She knew how much Emmalina's career meant to her and she would always call her when she went to Boston. The last we heard, Emmalina dressed herself like a little girl and would sit under the piano when anyone came to the house. I just couldn't believe it. We were all so depressed about it. Then, the last time Rosalind called, she said, "Who? Rosalind who? Andy who? Johnny who?" Maybe she was pretending. Maybe it was just one of her capers. You never knew. Over time, Rosalind and Emmalina had seemed to switch personalities. Rosalind was very quiet compared to Emmalina. Emmalina was outgoing and fun and so alive and interesting. Later I felt that Rosalind was taking on Emmalina's personality. She acted like her. She took on that persona. She became bubbly and her career really took off.

Rosalind is still at the Met. She has done every important mezzo soprano role. It was her life. She was committed. That's what it takes. You have to have that commitment. Without it, talent is nothing.

Now I have to tell you about Maureen McNally and me.

I know she was happily married to Claude Giroux for over forty years. I loved her for all of those forty years. They had five wonderful children. I will always love her, even though she's gone now.

I have to tell you what happened to me when I first saw her, but let me set the scene.

A coach at the Conservatory, Fred Popper, and his wife, wanted to rent a certain house in Brookline, just outside of Boston. They needed two people to help pay the rent. They asked me to come and see the place and meet their first roomer, a girl from Cleveland, Ohio. "A swell girl," Fred said.

He knew her from theater in Cleveland, where he coached her for the operas and operettas she worked in regularly. She was coming to study at the Conservatory. He thought I'd like the house and I did. It was handy to the Conservatory and beautiful. I said I'd move in the next day and at that moment, Maureen ran down the stairs. I was instantly bowled over, smitten, discombobulated and in love.

She was beautiful, with long, auburn hair and green eyes and white skin. But what struck me most was her joy. Such joy! Such a love of life.

She didn't fall in love with me, but we became fast friends. We worked together and laughed all the time. We lived mostly on pasta, so much so we finally had to go on diets. She had that fey quality that you sometimes find in Irish girls. She was always a little remote from what was going on, especially if she was having money troubles. It was appealing but it could get her in over her head. She had a lovely voice. I can still hear her singing "Over The Rainbow" at the grand piano in the Poppers' living room. I can never hear that song without seeing her just as she was, coming down the stairs, a true Irish beauty.

Maureen and I went to auditions like most young people today go to malls or the movies. We heard there was a call at the Latin Quarter in Boston for singers who could dance. Maureen had a lot of dance experience in the shows she did in Cleveland, and I had been studying dance and stage movement all the time I was in Boston. So we dressed up and appeared at the Quarter, to meet the director of the shows that were put on in their big room. His name was Johnny King. He was clearly Irish and all of eighteen years old, but he had the skill and temperament of a long-time producer and director.

Johnny instantly joined the ranks of Maureen's admirers. She sang "Over The Rainbow" for him, and I sang "Old Man River." He hired us both on the spot. He never asked us a question about our experience or training, though we tried to tell him. He didn't care. If he had the two of us in the show, he knew he had a hit. He thought I was pretty good too.

Things just happened for Maureen, mostly good things. We worked together and never had a fight or a bad word between us. It was a fabulous friendship. She came from a huge Irish family and had a strong Catholic upbringing. She would never wear clothes that might show off her figure. When she wasn't on stage, she never wore makeup and her street clothes could have been worn by any Catholic high school girl in America. She seemed alarmed by the effect her beauty had on everyone. She tried to hide it but did not succeed. She stopped traffic everywhere we went. I used to tell her she might as well dress up because all the men who saw her fell in love with her, even in what I called her "potato sacks."

She belonged in show business. She had that Mary Martin quality. You had to love her. She won every audition she ever went out for. But she had to go back to

Cleveland and work there until she could save enough money to come back to the Conservatory. Unfortunately, she didn't have the backing of her family in her career. I'll never understand that.

When Emmalina DeVita left "Tom, Dick & Carrie" and went to Europe, I sent for Maureen. Her letters to me had been one long repetition of "Get me out of here. I'm miserable. I want to get back to Boston." I called her and told her we had bookings for the act. They weren't paying that much, but if she wanted to try it, please come.

It was springtime and my last year of getting my master's, 1961. I had decided it was time to go to New York, full-time, with the act. Johnny King, Emmalina, and I had been earning money with it, and it was time to get a choreographer who did Broadway-level work. Maureen arrived. The three of us drove to New York in Johnny's convertible on weekends. We had a really classy set but no agent.

This was the time I changed my name from Santo, or Sandy, as my sisters called me, to Andy Thomas. I had chosen Thomas as my confirmation name and now decided Andy had a stronger sound than Sandy and the two names together would fit nicely on a marquee. Years later, Geraldine Fitzgerald got me to take back my family name, but that's another story.

Emmalina's costumes weren't a perfect fit for Maureen so we had them altered. I got my master's degree. I had been studying, teaching and performing wherever the bookings took me. That spring is now something of a blur to me. We left for New York immediately after graduation and found rooms at the Briarfield Hotel, Johnny and me in one room and Maureen with a room mate. The Briarfield was perfect: cheap, clean, on the West Side of Manhattan, and it had a switchboard where we could leave and get messages, have cleaning dropped off, all things essential to performers. There was a kitchenette where we could cook pasta and reheat leftovers. Heaven in the West Eighties! Mostly we lived on Chinese food. We immediately began looking for an agent. Johnny and Maureen visited agents who were known to accept new acts. I thought for a while and called my friend from Boston, Charlotte Shork Higgins, and Charlotte called Jack Talan of MCA, then the best agents in the country. He liked "Tom, Dick & Carrie," so the bookings began to roll in. Johnny remembers how flabbergasted he and Maureen were when I told him Jack Talan was our agent. "That's Andy," he told Maureen. "He starts at the top." Career-wise, we were set. Money was less of a problem. The three of us auditioned on our own whenever we could. We began to be known. Johnny was blond, I was brunette and Maureen was the spectacular performer in the middle. Our costumes were fresh and new, Johnny and I looked good, and Maureen acquired her usual train of adorers. Maureen and I had great voices and we were good dancers. Johnny had a good voice and was a great dancer.

What could go wrong?

The act was performing at the Astor Roof. An agent-entrepreneur, Barron Polan, saw us. He was famous for making stars out of girls like Julie Wilson and Jane Morgan. He had terrific respect in the business, so if he approved, the girl had to be good.

Barron Polan came backstage and said to Maureen, "I would like to put you up for Sarah Brown, the Salvation Army girl in *Guys and Dolls*. You're perfect for the part." She was perfect, but she got the understudy for Sarah. She left "Tom, Dick & Carrie."

That's what could go wrong.

Johnny and I always stayed in touch with Maureen. He's almost an uncle to the kids. When Maureen got sick, she had the best of care. Johnny and I love her just as much as we always did. Even though she's gone now.

Now it's time for Johnny King to tell you about those early years on Broadway. He remembers so much more than I do, that I think it's time you heard from him directly.

Johnny King may not be a famous man but he is a wonderful performer/teacher. Without him, I don't know what turn my career would have taken. He is now a director-choreographer at the Singers Forum. Men and women with his skills are the backbone of show business. Johnny has brought literally a thousand students on to our stage, calmed their nerves, answered their questions and transformed them from gawky, trembling, terrified stage virgins into sophisticated, fearless young performers.

I want him to tell the story of the early years of our friendship and careers because he has his own perspective and total recall. Johnny tells a story better than anyone I know so the "I" in this next chapter is Johnny himself.

IV

New York

By Johnny King

I met Andy in Boston in 1949, late in his senior year at the New England Conservatory of Music. I came from a show business family and I had been working at it since I was very young. I was a choreographer for Boston University and Tufts College student shows. I cast, wrote, directed, choreographed and danced in shows at Boston's Latin Quarter. One day, I was casting a Cole Porter revue at the Quarter and I was auditioning singers/dancers. A young couple came in to audition. He sang "Old Man River" and she sang "How Are Things In Gloccamora?" They handled themselves well on stage and sang beautifully. They were two total professionals. A director's dream. So I said to him, "How is it possible that you two can be students and be so wonderful? You know so much and are so experienced."

Well, it seemed Andy'd been working since he was a kid and Maureen was a leading lady in Cleveland with a huge résumé. So I hired them for the Cole Porter revue and they were just absolutely fabulous. In turn, they got me a lot of wonderful talent from the Conservatory. The show got raves because we had Cole Porter's music and the best talent in Boston.

In this show, Andy and Maureen and I did some numbers together. I was a dancer. They sang and danced. Then I had a dance concert coming up and hired them again. We did a trio number, then they would come out and sing. That was the beginning of a great friendship. The three of us became inseparable. Maureen was my darling, too.

Maureen wanted passionately to do opera and began to concentrate on her repertoire, so Andy and I began to work with Emmalina DeVita, who was part of "Musical Portraits," the act that Andy put together earlier with Dana Lordly, to earn enough money to stay in Boston.

Our act with Emmalina was very different. We called ourselves "Tom, Dick & Carrie." I staged it and it was just like magic. We never had to worry about selling ourselves. We went into the Balinese Room in Boston, and the Copley Plaza. "Tom, Dick & Carrie" just took off. It wasn't what you'd call a harmony act. It was more like a little staged revue with three people. We did things from *The Wizard of Oz*. Andy was the Tin Man and I was the Scarecrow. Emmalina was Dorothy. She was a very talented, beautiful girl. In the meantime, Maureen had gone home to Cleveland because she ran out of money. She could work there in opera and save money living at home. Emmalina, Andy and I continued with the act and it became very successful. We began to think of branching out into New York City.

Emmalina looked like Brigitte Bardot, really. But she was a character. Once she told us her father covered her bed with rose petals, with her in it. Not a good sign, but how were we to know? We thought her wild stunts were just diva stuff, being a prima donna. We didn't realize how child-like she was. After a really ghastly stunt, Andy and I would say, "We're not going to speak to that girl for the rest of our lives!" And the next minute we'd be

57

forgiving her. Once we worked in a very elegant room, and they fed us before the show. Emmalina wouldn't dress for dinner, so we'd try to go to the dining room before her. We would huddle together in the back of the room, behind menus. The whole place would be dressed to the nines with diamonds and haute couture and she would come in with a terrible skirt and blouse and her hair would be in curlers. Instead of coming in quietly, she'd go, "Oh, oh, oh!" and make an entrance like an opera singer coming on stage. And she'd head straight for us.

We went to the theater one night with Emmalina. We were sitting in the second balcony when Andy said, "Oh, there's an empty box available."

I said, "You guys go. I don't want to."

Andy said, "Oh, come on, don't be chicken."

I said, "Okay, we'll just sneak into the box quietly."

Emmalina stepped in front and made this big entrance. The whole audience stared at us. I died! But in a way, she was right, because nobody would ever think you were sneaking in that way.

Andy was always doing things like that. Once, the two of us went to see Ruth Draper. Again, we were up in the balcony. Andy said, "Look, down there—only two people in that whole second row. Lots of seats vacant! Let's go."

I said, "Nothing could go wrong with a whole row." So we sat down in two seats at the end and just before Miss Draper came on, the man in one of the two occupied seats came over to us and said, "You're sitting in my row."

Andy said, "You mean you have the whole row?"

The man said, "Yes, I bought out the whole row. My wife and I don't want anybody else in our row."

Andy said, "You're not going to let a couple of students sit here?"

The man answered, "No. This is my row."

So we got thrown out of those seats and had to walk back through the whole house. I was terribly embarrassed. It was awful. But it was helpful to me in a way. I was forced to be embarrassed, a thing I avoided like the plague, and I survived.

Once we got started with the trio, we had to pay for Emmalina's wardrobe and our own. She had to take care of it because we couldn't be buying new dresses every week. We were booked into a hotel in Nassau, in the Bahamas. In order to get there, we found a booking on a cruise ship. We had to do one show on the way down, get off the ship, do our booking at the hotel, get back on the ship on its return to New York, and do another show. That was our transportation. The moment we got on the ship, Emmalina said, "I don't think I'll be able to do the show." Those were her first words. We would have to pay for tickets if we didn't do the show and we did not have that kind of money, because Emmalina had just gotten two new dresses for the act. One of them was from a bridal shop. Emmalina had asked us to come and okay the dress. There she was, a bride? She had had a hoop put in the skirt of the dress. We didn't know it, but every time we moved toward her, the skirt would fly up. That meant we weren't able to get to the mike at all. And we had bought her another dress. I told her we had to do the show. She got a shot from the ship's doctor and now she was feeling terrific, in one of her brand new outfits. We did the act, and Andy sang, "When you walk through a storm, hold your head up high . . ." and he was green. I was, too. Then Emmalina turned green. I don't know how we got through the act, but we did. The ocean calmed down a bit and we all felt better. Andy said to Emmalina, "I think you'd better take off the dress because you're going to wear it New

Year's Eve at the hotel. Go down and take it off."

"Oh, no, if I go downstairs I'm going to get seasick again. Don't worry, I'm fine," said Emmalina, and she walked by the buffet and saw all this food and threw up all over herself and the new two hundred and fifty dollar dress.

So one new dress was out. She only had two outfits and Andy and I had several changes, so we had to reconceive the costuming.

Emmalina was always afraid to be alone when we were on the road, so when I said to Andy, "I'm taking our shirts to the laundry," Emmalina said, "Oh, would you take something for me?" I said, "Sure." She handed me a package. I went to the cleaner and he opened the package and it's the dress she threw up on. It was a horrible sight. What a look that man gave me. The dress was never the same after that.

Rosalind and Emmalina were a study in contrasts. Emmalina was a bit neurotic. We used to laugh about it together, Rosalind, Andy and I. We all thought she was being a diva, acting up and carrying on. Something wasn't quite right. If attention wasn't being paid to her, we had problems. She was spoiled. Her father, particularly, doted on her. She told us he would come into her bedroom and throw rose petals on her bed. We had no idea of the implications of his behavior to her. She was so beautiful. She looked like the young Brigitte Bardot. In his last year at the Conservatory, Andy, Emmalina and I were doing an act we called "Tom, Dick & Carrie." We were booked in the big room on a cruise ship. We were just about to go on when Emmalina decided to shave under her arms. She was wearing a strapless dress. When she came out of her dressing room, she was bleeding. She said, "I'll take care of it," and put Kleenex tissues in her underarms. She stood there with her arms close to her body while we waited in the wings to go on. Our opening number was "One Of The Roving Kind," and it had big moves. We ran out on stage and we all flung our arms in the air and started to sing, while the Kleenex fluttered to the floor. She didn't pay any attention to it. I don't know how Andy and I managed to do the number. That's the kind of thing Emmalina would do. She was wild, but she was wonderful.

Now we were down to the wedding dress with the hoop in it. Every time we'd sing, we'd get close to Emmalina to get to the mike—and her skirt would fly up. Think of Carol Burnett's version of *Gone With The Wind*. Andy would push the hoop down from his side and the other side would go up. And she wore wedgies with it. Every time the skirt would go up, there would be those awful wedgies.

But, oh, what a voice she had!

Later on in Nassau, we got to know this one man who was in show business and he said, "I've seen your act seven or eight times."

Andy said, "Oh, that's wonderful. You must love it."

The man said, "No, I just want to see what's going to happen next!"

Thank God, Emmalina decided she didn't want to do "Tom, Dick & Carrie" any longer. She told us she was going to Europe to be a diva. Andy called Maureen McNally in Cleveland and said we needed her. She could make enough to live on and be in New York, where the action was. Maureen joined us in New York. We were in the city full time, no more driving back and forth on weekends from Boston to New York. We lived at a hotel on the Upper West Side, the Briarfield. We had our own Boston crowd: Rosalind Elias, Willabelle Underwood,

Joan Moynaugh, Maureen, Andy and me.

First, Maureen, Andy and I needed an agent for the act. We divvied up the work of seeing agents. Maureen and I were starting small because we figured you don't start out in the Empire Room or the Starlight Roof of the Waldorf Astoria. So we began seeing little agents. We'd come back each day and we'd say to each other, "Well, who did you see?" Andy would say, "Well, I was at the William Morris office. Then I went to MCA." These were the two biggest and best agents in the business. We would say, "You're really cracking up." (P.S. He got us an audition with Jack Talan at MCA. Jack took us on and that was the beginning.) We just did the act as long as we wanted to.

That was the beginning of a very successful time for us, in the early years of television. We did TV shows. We did "Chance of A Lifetime" and all kinds of wonderful shows. We started playing all over the country: Chicago, at the Edgewater Beach Hotel, the Blue Room in New Orleans, the Monteleone in New Orleans; the very top spots. It was a great time.

Maureen always dressed down when she wasn't on stage. She was the most gorgeous girl I ever saw in my life. She would wear an old skirt and blouse and tie her hair back and wear no makeup. We'd constantly try to get her to keep on her stage makeup and dress up so we could go out with her after the show and be seen. I couldn't figure her out. I once said to her brother, "Boy, your sister was so gorgeous!"

He said to me, "Yeah, and thank God she didn't know it." They considered makeup and dressy clothes to be loose behavior. It was a very Catholic family.

She would never show anything below her chin, even on stage. She'd wear a little bib tucked in any low neckline. We were doing a show, the hundredth anniversary of something, and they told us we would be handed a cake during our act. In the middle of the act, a lady came up with the cake, candles already lit. We made a little speech. She handed the lit cake to Maureen, and the bib in her cleavage caught fire. We knocked the cake out of her hands and pulled the bib off her chest. Later, I said, to a slightly singed Maureen, "God is telling you something. You're not meant to wear that bib. It's dangerous."

Maureen was our friend for her whole life. I've always lived almost next door to her and her family. She eventually had five kids, and I love them like my own. Andy's phone call to Maureen, to bring her to New York, changed her life. She married a wonderful man who was rich enough to see that she was taken care of in their home, to the very end, when she suffered from Alzheimer's. She had nurses round the clock. Her children and friends were able to be with her constantly. She didn't speak much in the last year of her life, but once, when I told her Andy was coming, she said, clearly, "Oh, he's such a nice man!" I prayed every day for a cure, but my prayers weren't answered.

We did have one big problem with the act. Any girl that worked between us had the greatest showcase in the world. We were fairly good looking guys. We always focused the material on the girl. The problem was that their looks and their talent would get spotted, and off they'd go. Barron Polan spotted Maureen, took her out of the act and put her into *Guys and Dolls,* as Sarah Brown's understudy, then into *Carousel* with John Raitt. Another girl was spotted by George Abbott. And on it went. Andy and I got tired of breaking in new girls, buying them wardrobes and then watching them wave goodbye.

There was one very strange "Carrie" toward the end.

We watched her pick guys up, right off the stage, during the act. She was missing one night and we were ready to go on. We didn't know where she was. I knocked on her door and told her we were ready. She didn't respond so I opened the door. Her bra, her panties, her dress, everything was there. I said, "Andy, did you check the parking lot?" She was out there in a car with some guy, in her coat, with nothing on underneath it.

Andy and I finally decided to give up the act and go out on our own. We were ready to step out of the showcase it provided us, and in the very beginning, we had agreed that if either of us got a good gig, we could go on and do it.

Andy and I roomed together. Money was tight. We were used to each other's foibles. He was friendly with a very wealthy woman and her debutante daughter. They lived on Park Avenue, at 57th Street, next door to Marlon Brando, who always played his bongos night and day, and was driving them nuts. One day, Andy said, "Oh, by the way, I'm taking so-and-so to the Debutante Ball at the Waldorf."

I said, "On what?"

He said, "I'm taking her."

I said to him. "Andy, number one, you have to go to Twenty-One or the Stork Club afterward. You don't just go to the Debutante Ball. It's their big night. They expect to be taken out, to be seen!"

Andy said, "Don't worry." Later, he asked me, "How much have you got?"

I said, "About three bucks."

He said, "That'll help. I'll take it."

So he took my three bucks and I think he had three bucks and he went to his piggy bank and took out a bunch of pennies. He told me later that the girl came down, dressed to the nines. Andy was in his working tuxedo with six bucks in his pocket plus a lot of pennies. Right away, they had to take a cab from 57th to the Waldorf Astoria. At that time, it cost about a dollar, plus tip. Andy gave the driver the pennies for a tip and the guy rolled down his window, said, "Keep your God damn pennies!" and threw them into the street.

Andy told me he said to his date, "How do you like that? They don't even take pennies these days!"

I asked him what happened after the Ball. He told me she said, "Let's go to the Stork Club!"

He said, "Oh, no, not that. I hate nightclubs. I work in them all the time. Let's go to your place and make some eggs. We'll have a good time!" That's how he survived the evening. I wouldn't have gone. I did not have the guts.

While we lived at the Briarfield, our gang of Bostonians had an unwritten agreement that whoever was working brought home a cake. Once Andy was working in *Golden Apple.* So he would bring home cake every night after work, something to have in our apartment, the only one with a stove. We could make coffee. The switchboard person would call everyone up and say, "He's home! Yes, everybody, he's home!" Everyone would march into the apartment and we'd have a midnight feast. The girls would come in robes, pajamas and slippers, with curlers in their hair. We talked over the day's adventures and kept each other's hopes up, while we devoured Andy's cake.

Roz Elias made it to the Metropolitan Opera. Willabelle Underwood went to the New York City Opera. Before she did, Andy tried to get her into *Golden Apple.* She was a tall soprano. He got her all dolled up in someone else's dress and she looked gorgeous. Vocally, she was right for the part but she dwarfed the leading man so they couldn't use her opposite him.

In those days, you could park a car in the city without

having to buy the street. I had a car, a convertible, that my dad had given me while I lived in Boston. It came in handy for all of us. One day, Andy called me and said, "Oh, Johnny, I just met a Miss Rheingold contestant. You know, Rheingold Beer?"

I said, "Oh, nice. Wonderful."

He said, "We're going out tonight. I don't have much money so I told her, 'Bring along a friend for my friend.'"

I said, "Andy, I'll do it on one condition, that when we get in the car, we drive out to Coney Island. We'll have hot dogs. There's no money here. Just don't make any statements. Promise!" So we picked up these two visions, beautiful girls in cocktail dresses, matching shoes and bags, earrings, the lot. After hello, the first thing I said was, "We're going to Coney Island. Would you like the top down?"

Andy got in the back with his date and the first words out of his mouth were, "Where do you want to go, girls?"

"Bill Miller's Riviera," they answered, together. I had a few bucks in my pocket. Andy had change for the bridge. I panicked. We went to Bill Miller's Riviera. The girls ordered steaks. We said we weren't hungry, so we had water and bread. The girls hardly looked at us, they were so busy checking out the room to see who was there. When they went to the ladies' room, I said, "Andy, how are we going to pay for this?"

Andy said, "Oh, come on, I know you've got some money. You take care of it."

I said, "Andy, I have no money on me." Five dollars had already gone to the parking lot attendant. If we had seven dollars between us, it would be a miracle. I thought I must be having a nightmare. It couldn't be true. In the hottest spot in town, I'm trying to stiff the management!

All of a sudden, out of the blue, I remembered something. When I left home, two years earlier, my dad had said, "I put a check in the ashtray of your car in case of an emergency." This was an emergency, all right. I ran out to the car, pulled the ashtray out, and there was the check! My dad's check. We paid our bill with it and had a great time. God always took care of me. I don't know, to this day, what made Andy say, "Where would you like to go, girls?" I do remember that Peter Lind Hayes and Mary Healy were the main act.

Andy set me up so many times, but it always worked out. At his invitation, we'd all go to the movies. "There's a great movie," he'd say. We'd all have to go to Loew's 83rd, right? We'd get to the movie with Roz and Willabelle. None of us were working. We'd line up for tickets, Andy standing apart from us. One of us would say, "Andy, aren't you going to get in line?" He would answer, "I don't have enough money." Roz would say, "But you invited us to the movies. What do you mean, you don't have any money?" Andy would say, "I guess I just won't be able to go," I'd find a quarter, Roz fifteen cents, Willa a dime. We'd raise enough to get him into the movie, at his invitation.

He never seemed to feel poor, and he never acted poor. Somehow it always worked out.

Once, the trio worked Ben Maksik's place in Brooklyn, New York. We opened for the headliner, Buddy Hackett. Buddy was not doing business. Ben came back to our dressing room and said, "If you guys don't start bringing in the people, I'm going to fire you." Can you imagine wanting three kids to draw the people? Buddy was supposed to be the draw. We weren't getting paid that much. So Andy said to Ben, pointing at me, "Do you know who his father is?

Ben said, "No."

Andy said, "Well, I wouldn't advise you to fire him!"

He was implying that my dad was Irish Mafia. Ben left us alone after that.

One of those times between jobs, Andy was looking for work. He went to Brooklyn and auditioned for a club in the afternoon. He sang and they loved him. By the way, Andy has without a doubt one of the most natural voices I've ever heard in my life. It's one of those Italian *bel canto* voices, a wonderful sound. No matter what happens, he can stand up and sing, any time, anywhere, any music. Back to my point: the club was called the Ridgewood Terrace. He went to work that night, in his tuxedo, and he did a very classy act, "Mack the Knife" and all that good stuff. He discovered he was the only legitimate act on the bill. There were strippers, midgets who told dirty jokes, transvestites—a raunchy, dirty show. I couldn't believe it. Andy came on and just killed the people, who had more or less ignored the rest of the show. Everybody on Broadway came to see Andy. Charles Nelson Reilly and Bobby Morse, who were friends of his, brought all their other friends. We were always packed, in spite of the rest of the show. Not only did Andy wear a tuxedo, he always had a fresh boutonniere in his lapel. He wasn't touched by the decadence. But you took whatever job you could get. That's the business. You could be working the best club in town one week, and the next week you'd be in some basement joint. You had to keep money coming in.

I used to tease Andy all the time. We'd be out somewhere, and I'd go to the men's room and come back and say, "Oh, you know who was in the men's room? Richard Rodgers!" and he'd go flying into the men's room, singing "Some Enchanted Evening." Of course, Richard Rodgers wouldn't be there.

I was still rooming with Andy when he was production singer at the Copacabana. They had two shows a night and three on Saturdays. The Copa was the hottest club in town. Eight o'clock, ten o'clock, and two o'clock in the morning on Saturdays. Andy didn't get home till three-thirty in the morning. I don't remember if he had a night off that whole year. I'd be in my room, sound asleep. Andy would come in and say to me, "Johnny? Are you awake?"

I'd say, "No."

He'd say, "Guess who was in the club tonight."

I'd say, "I don't know. Who was in the club tonight?"

He'd say, "Lena Horne." Or, "Frank Sinatra." Always big celebrities, big, big, big names, came to see the show. Andy was there for a year. Every night he had a new list of celebrities. But as the year went on, they got less and less important.

Finally, one night, he came in and said, "Are you awake?"

"No."

"Guess who was in the club tonight."

"I don't know."

After a long pause, he said, "Gaby Hayes."

Andy and I nearly laughed ourselves sick. We knew that was the end of the celebrities in that engagement. Everybody had seen the show. Andy had to come up with somebody, so for the younger generation, Gaby Hayes played a movie cowboy with a beard and no teeth for his whole career. Everybody knew him then. His character was a standing joke in the business.

As a trio, Andy, Maureen and I had made very good money. Even with the replacements, we were a great commodity. When we gave up the trio, we had to start from the beginning. We had to make the rounds. It was a hard time. We had to pay the rent so we took every job we could.

Andy knew what struggle was. He came to Boston with a hundred dollars in his pocket and a partial scholarship. What good was a hundred dollars, even then? You could live a month, maybe. So you can imagine what it took for him to survive. The jobs he had to take, bus boy, waiter, stock boy . . . He was twenty-one years old when he came to Boston. He got a church job. He formed the "Musical Portraits" trio with Emmalina DeVita and Dana Lordly. He took club jobs. After we became friends, he would show up at my house at five o'clock, for dinner. That took care of his evening meal. It's funny, the things you remember. Andy had to work hard. His family could help only a little. I envied him his parents, more than I ever envied anybody in my life. If I had my choice of a mother, it would be Loretta, Andy's mother. And his father was a dream person. When we would pass through Buffalo on our way to a job in Canada, Andy's dad would get up early in the morning and make us breakfast. I never saw my dad do anything like that. We never demonstrated affection, my dad and I. Loretta would just embrace you. She was the best.

You'd buy Loretta a little cup and saucer and it would be the most important thing in her life. I learned so much from her. I think a lot of what Andy inherited was from his mother. She was a survivor.

With Loretta, everything was wonderful. Even when it was bad, it was wonderful. Just like Andy. Once Andy was away and I was helping to supervise a paint job in his apartment. His mother was there. She had the painters moving the sofa she sat on from room to room because with every brush stroke, she would say, "Oh, that's wonderful, honey! This is the best paint job I've ever seen." The painters loved her. They couldn't wait to put another brush stroke on the walls. That paint job has lasted all these years.

She was very attractive and was up on all the latest about everything. Nothing but goodness in her. She was so sweet, such a sweet lady.

My thing with Loretta was, whenever she came to town, we had a date. I would take her to bingo. For a while, it was very important that she win. She had very little money. Once Andy was successful, we took her shopping. Her favorite shop was B. Altman's Town Shop. Then we went to bingo. And lost. On the way, she said, "Oh, that's all right, honey, Thank God we don't need it!"

Andy's father looked like Errol Flynn. He was beautiful, the handsomest guy you ever saw in your life. He was completely unaware of it. Like Maureen McNally was unaware of her beauty.

When I was rooming with Andy, if Al came to town, the first thing he would do was check the furniture. "That's a little tattered. I'm sure it's a little tattered," would be his first words. Then he would say, "Is there a hardware store nearby?" He would go and get some little tacks and find a fabric store and get a piece of material. He'd put the little tacks between his teeth and reupholster the chair. Right on the spot. I was fascinated by him. He was a straight-up guy, no baloney. He was a natural athlete. He played on a baseball team and ran races. What made Andy was the combination of two positive parents. They were so far ahead of their time. Neither believed in hitting their children, an attitude still viewed with suspicion by many parents to this day. You don't have to have a lot of money to turn out three fabulous kids, which they did. That father of Andy's drove him all over town to all his dates. He was an incredible man and as far as I'm concerned, an extremely successful man. Success is not measured by the money you make in life.

71

It's judged by what you accomplish as a person, I believe, and what you give to the next generation.

I'm sure they never made Andy feel that he was poor. He wouldn't see it that way. He would find a way of changing it, turning it around. I never heard Loretta or Angelo crying about money. They'd go to the farm in the country. They worked the farm with Loretta's father, all of them. They didn't have money but they had everything you could get from a farm. Loretta canned and cooked and baked. It was really a wonderful place. All we had to do was cross the road to swim in Lake Erie. Wonderful characters lived in the neighborhood and they were all friends.

I never had to struggle. I think God took care of Andy, but somebody, some human being, always took care of me. I was adopted by Guy Sweeney and lived a very comfortable life. I would never have left Boston if I hadn't met Andy and joined the trio. We would never have had the trio if my father hadn't had the money to set the trio up. Among the three of us we had no cash. Andy had to drag me out of Boston. I had never planned to perform. I wanted to stage the shows. And here's the funny part: what I started out to do in Boston, I'm now doing at Andy's school, the Singers Forum, in New York. I wanted to be a director/producer, director/choreographer. And I went through a whole career as a performer to come back to being a director/choreographer. It all worked out.

We rode on Andy's coat tails. Maureen and I. We had talent, but not like Andy's. He would do anything. We had to practice, practice, practice. We didn't have Andy's drive. He was a human tornado. He had drive and intelligence and he moved us up each step of the ladder by pushing and pulling and ranting and raving. I didn't have his drive, his passion for the work. I thought you got discovered in a drugstore, sitting on a stool, like Lana Turner. Andy connected with everyone, like when he found Jack Talan at MCA. He gave back in full measure. Jack loved his drive. People used to say to Andy, "You'll make it. You've got the drive." And he had a winning personality. He had balls. My problem was always fear of rejection. I was an adopted child. Somebody had given me away. Now I see it for what it's worth. Rejection is nothing. You handle it. Andy wouldn't allow me to be afraid of being rejected.

Andy recognizes talent. He always has. He loves talent. He knows you have to fail a lot, to work without letup, no matter how much talent you have.

It's been a great ride, and I'm seventy plus and still working. Because of Andy.

Let me tell you a little about the Singers Forum. It's amazing, the student body at the school. Some students have no intention ever to sing professionally. Many schools won't take students without that kind of ambition. And this is the first school I've ever seen where students actually get up and sing every time they come to class. You have to do that. You have to get up and sing. That's how you get over your nerves. You can't just sit in the audience and think about it. Schools I've been to, you're lucky if you get up once a month. You should see how confident our students are. And the professional students tell me they learn a lot from the very beginning about what not to do.

I realize my career couldn't happen today. It can cost thousands of dollars a year just to go to school. There are no little clubs to pay the rent for people coming up today. Students ask, "What can we do to gain experience?" The only way now is to come to class as often as you can. At least you're singing here, in front of an audience. You're learning by getting up and doing it. Do charity shows, concerts at senior citizen centers, at hospitals. Never say no! I do a "Put Your Act Together" class. I ask what kind of act students want to do. Once you've settled on that, take every opportunity to work that comes your way. Do weddings, funerals, birthday parties. You don't start at the Metropolitan Opera or Yankee Stadium. You start here, in front of your peers, and you learn your craft.

Great Students

Tony Bennett

There was a point in his career when Tony Bennett changed, in the early 60s. He really opened up and got free in a way he never was before. The reviewers picked it up. I had to go and see him at the Copa because I'd always liked him. I was astounded by the change. Everybody was talking about it.

Of all the pop singers, I think he was my favorite. I was stunned by his freedom and the absolute change in this man. The reviewers said he had been working with somebody, not just a coach, not just a therapist, but someone who was both. I said, "God, I've got to meet this person." In Ed Sullivan's column one day there was an item about Tony and that the man responsible for his new personality was Michael Brown, and that he and his wife had just had a baby. I went immediately to the phone book and found Michael Browns and called them all. I said, "Are you the Michael Brown who is responsible for Tony Bennett?" Finally, one said, "Yes." I said, "I just want to tell you I have never seen such a change in anyone like what has happened to him. It's just the most marvelous thing. I've got to meet you. I've got to talk to you because I feel that Tony's and my backgrounds are very similar and I want to know what it was that brought this kind of freedom into his life." He said, "Well, I'd like to meet you, too, because you're the only one who's called."

We did meet. Michael Brown was a wonderful man, a therapist and an acting coach. He combined both skills in his classes. He told me to read a book called, *The Art Of Loving,* by Eric Fromm. He made Tony read it and it really helped him to make the change.

The Art of Loving was my ticket to a new aspect of metaphysics, to that kind of philosophical thinking. I was very moved by that book.

When I met Michael, I felt we had made a connection. I went to some of his classes. I don't remember if I wasn't ready for it or I didn't have the money to continue working with him, but what I found out helped me into heavy metaphysical thinking. Michael Brown was very important to me; and Tony, without knowing it, was very important to me, too.

A few years later, Tony and I were working in Framingham, Massachusetts, on opposite sides of the street, me at Vaughn Monroe's Meadows, and Tony at the Monticello. I went over when I thought he would be rehearsing and spoke to him. I told him about me and Michael and *The Art of Loving.* He thought that was just wonderful. I said, "It just seems so coincidental that we're here in this town, across the street from one another. Would you mind if I came to your show?" My shows were at different times from his. He said, "Of course, come any time you want." He would come over to the Meadows and have an early dinner with me before the shows, every night for two weeks. I was in such awe of him. He came over to see one of my shows. We just had the greatest time. He told me a lot of stories about his career. He was so direct, so with his feet on the ground. He seemed to be just an ordinary man, as Professor Higgins says in *My Fair Lady.* On stage, Tony was not an ordinary man. The fact that he achieved what he did, and is still achieving it now, in his mid-seventies, is not ordinary. It's because his creativity is always open to growth. He paints very well, and he sells his paintings. He said, "You have to keep it up. You always have to study. Always."

Some thirty-odd years later, I was invited by a student, Jerry King, to go with him to the Italian-American Awards dinner in Washington, D.C., on the third weekend in October, 1995. We were to be the guests of Dow Corning. It was all set that I was going, and then it dawned on me that Tony would be there. This made it double important to go. I would find a way to meet him again and talk to him. That September, Billy Stritch and Liza Minnelli had done a show with Tony, and Billy told me Tony said to him, "Every time I hear you, you get better and better. Who is your teacher?" So Billy told him I was his teacher. Tony said, "I have to meet this man."

At the dinner, awards went to Tony, Joe Montana and John Travolta, among others, The place was mobbed. President Clinton was there. He made the most fantastic speech. Hillary Clinton looked beautiful. They just took the place by storm. There were three thousand people there, all sitting at tables. You could hardly get through to talk to anyone. I thought, *How the hell am I going to get up to the dais and speak to Tony?* Mrs. Sergio Franchi was there, sitting at a very important table. I told Jerry I wanted to get some of these people interested in the Singers Forum. They give a lot of scholarships. I had told her I was coming when we spoke but now I couldn't get to her. Every time we started out, over the loudspeaker would come: "Everybody, please take your seats," and then it was time for this or that speech or award or message.

But then, at one point (Jerry can't get over how these things happen to me; he's just fascinated by it) all the nominees left the stage. But where did they go? I said, "Let's find them." We went behind the dais. There was a curtain pulled all the way across and there were body-guards—Secret Servicemen—all over the place. I went up to one and said, "Will Tony Bennett be coming this way? When I saw the curtain I thought they would be on the walkway back here."

This man said, "Yes."

I said, "Well, I have a message for him from Liza Min-nelli. Is there a way I could speak to him?" The guard said, "Why don't you stay right here? I'll tell you when they're coming back to the dais."

So Jerry and I waited about ten or fifteen minutes. They had gone backstage to meet the President in a pri-vate room! I couldn't have picked a better time to talk to Tony. He was so high, so up from talking with the Presi-dent. He and his girlfriend walked by and I said, "Tony, you just performed with two of my students and I wanted to say hello to you. I'm Andy Anselmo, and Liza Minnelli and Billy Stritch are my students."

Tony said, "We were talking about you. I gotta know what you do. I'd like to call you and come up and do some-thing."

I said, "That would be great!"

The way I feel about him has always been so positive. I loved this man's work over all these years. He didn't remember that we'd met before. I didn't bring that up. We had a nice, very brief chat. I gave him my card and said, "Call me and we'll do some scales and stuff." He said, "Do you teach *bel canto*?"

I said, "Of course. My teacher was the master teacher of Eleanor Steber in the *bel canto*."

There was no time for anything else. A bit later, I went to the men's room. Tony was there so I got to talk to him again. He said, "You've always gotta keep working and getting better. You have to work on your voice. You have to keep it up."

I said, "You're absolutely right."

He left and while I was washing up, there were two men there, politicians, and one said, "I never thought I'd be sharing a urinal with Tony Bennett." I said, "When it comes to a call of nature, we are all the same."

When I came out, I said, to Jerry, "You won't believe who was in the men's room." He just couldn't get over it.

When I got back to New York, exhausted as I was, I couldn't wait to tell Billy that I spoke to Tony. I said, "If he comes—or *when* he comes—it will be worth the fatigue I feel now that I'm home."

Surprise! A few months later, he did call and I went to see him. The teaching experience was and continues to be, exciting and fulfilling.

I must say that working with Tony really has had a big effect on me, not only professionally but personally. He is such a low-key, almost Zen-like person. It's that quality that really gets to people. There's no big show-biz ego there. It's really marvelous. At that first lesson, he was very open and listened and tried to do what we were talking about. He really understands what being a student is. He had a teacher in painting. He said he's getting a teacher to learn piano. I said, "That's good. You'll enjoy having a teacher for singing." He's always growing, always moving toward something.

It's difficult when you're working with someone like Tony Bennett, who's been singing all these years and is so successful at it, and you have to say, "Well, let's see how we can improve your voice." It's full of pressure. How do you say it? How do you get someone who hasn't had much formal training and is very used to what he does, to do it differently? I said to him, "Please don't judge anything. Just kind of do it and see what happens. I would like to know this isn't the only lesson. I hope we'll have two or three now, so that you can understand and see something happening. Then you'll know. But it's a lot of pressure on me in one lesson." He said he understood that. The problem was he was going to Philadelphia and then he was doing the Golden Globe Awards. He took a tape with him and worked with that. He is a realist and he works hard at his arts, harder than you would expect a man of his standing to do. He just loves the work.

He couldn't get over my energy. He was floored. He said, "Boy, I think it's just great, the way you look." I said, "I still hold on to my voice. I hope that you know I have loved your work for so long that it would make me really happy if I could help you to sing for another hundred years."

He has this white Maltese dog, a female, and he had to sing holding her the whole time because she insisted on staying with him. He said, "When we're alone, she's never like this, but when somebody else comes, she just goes right to me." She goes with him everywhere. She's so small, he can put her in a carrier and take her on the plane with him. She seemed very sweet-natured, not like my Dachshund, Giacomo, who is a survivor of abuse when a puppy and not very trusting.

Tony's is the most beautiful apartment I've ever seen. I would love living in that building. As you walk in, the lobby is fantastic. It's a fairly new building on Central Park. Tony said, "When I look out here I feel I'm in the country. I feel that I'm relaxed. I need that."

I told him that's why I had my little log cabin out in Sherman, Connecticut, for that very reason. Then Tony gave me the tour. The living room is huge, with tall, white columns, two or three of them. He's got a studio where he paints, with great north light. He has a Bosendorfer, the greatest piano ever built, and it's probably worth a mint.

During the lesson, he got some wonderful vocal sounds. They were very free, very open, very clear. There was no fatigue, no raspiness or anything like that. He does two hundred dates a year. That's the way it is when you're as hot as he is. It was wonderful, exciting, pleasurable, but always, when I leave, I wonder, *Will I ever do this again?* I hate that part of it. I tried to get him to see that we had to do this a few times for him to hear what could happen. I reminded him that he's crazy about Billy Stritch's voice.

I have to say he was bemused by the warmup position, standing, bent over, feet apart, head hanging down as far as it will go. It makes the cover automatically come into being. The sounds you make are different from when you're standing upright. It's the placement of the palate that makes the difference. I said, "This is what you do when you're warming up. It's a way to get the muscles to start working, but you don't have to bend over when you sing!" He laughed.

I found that first session equally tension-producing and rewarding. It was a wonderful experience because Tony was really the man who, through Michael Brown, started me on to a new level of metaphysics. I didn't want it to end. Maybe that was part of the let-down. It's hard to go back to regular life and regular teaching. Working with professionals is gratifying on many different levels.

Before I left, I said, "You've made my birthday a happy one." That's when we got into the age thing. He said, "Oh, my God, this is amazing." He looks wonderful himself. In fact, he looks better than ever.

A lot of things have come to me from Tony Bennett,

unbeknownst to him. I didn't go into that part of it with him then. I think he should know the effect he has on people. It's more than just entertaining them. He inspires them to work, to study, to achieve.

Jose Ferrer

When Jose Ferrer became president of the Players Club, I had been a long-time member. I was very excited about that because I thought he had the most beautiful speaking voice I'd ever heard. It was the texture of silk velvet and he had the ability to use it as a musical instrument. Once you heard Jose Ferrer speak, you never forgot his voice.

Jose told me he would love to sing, so whenever we were at the Club, I would urge him to come for a singing lesson.

At different times, he talked of his thirty-five voice teachers, of his studies in England, France and Italy. Wherever he went, he tried to find a teacher who could help him. He said, "I'd rather have been a singer than an actor. Most of my friends are singers." He was very friendly with Ezio Pinza, the great basso, and all the leading singers at the Metropolitan Opera. He just loved singers and singing.

Finally, one day, I said to him, "I know I can teach you how to sing. Let me give you a lesson as a present for your birthday." I hoped he didn't think I was in need of students, or that I was being pushy. (Sometimes I am pushy, but this wasn't one of them.) I said, "For someone who loves singing as much as you do, the time has come for you to learn how to do it. Let me give it a shot. Come to my house."

One afternoon, he breezed in before I could put my third Dachshund, Giacomo, on the leash. I always did because he was very suspicious of strangers. Jose had such enormous energy. It accompanied him like a giant wave. He went straight to Giacomo and played with him. Giacomo adored him from that moment forward. It didn't hurt that later on, Jose always came with a dog treat, and cuddled him.

I gave Jose his first lesson. We skipped the meditation and controlled breathing because his actor's training had given him all that. I showed him how to bend over and relax his upper body, his arms, hands and facial muscles. I sat down at the piano and played the middle C scale and sang it for him. Then I told him to breathe deeply and sing the sounds EEE OH NO, on pitch, head down, through the whole scale, then begin at the bottom note again and straighten up slowly. As he did, this enormous, beautiful sound came out of his entire body.

He stopped and said, "Oh, my God! I've never made a sound like that!"

I told him, "When you're in that position, bending over, you breathe all the way to your back. The soft palate goes up, the larynx drops down, the root of the tongue pulls it down, and your throat is wide open."

Jose said, "You won't believe this, but I was born without a soft palate. My parents took me from Puerto Rico to New York City to have an operation when I was a little boy. It gave me a soft palate so that I could learn to speak properly. I don't know how it was done."

I said, "Well, your soft palate is lazy because it's not a true muscle. Unless you really pull it up, it won't work. The position you were in pulled it up naturally, so you could make that huge, wonderful sound. I'm glad you told me because now I know what we're dealing with."

I never saw a happier man in my whole life. From then on, we had the most solid friendship. He told everyone about me. He sang in the great musical, *Fanny,* on Broadway. He sang in a new production with Mandy Patinkin, in Edinburgh. It was really an opera. He sang the role of Scarpia in the second act of "Tosca" with Carol Wilcock, a wonderful student of John Harris's and mine, at the Singers Forum. It was his dream role.

I know that learning to sing made the last three years of Jose's life really happy. He fulfilled his lifelong ambition, his dream role.

All his life he used his voice for the utmost good, after having been born without a soft palate. I'm so glad I could give him the only thing he really wanted: a beautiful singing voice.

In May of '99, Stella Ferrer, Jose's widow, called me from her home in Florida to say she was coming to New York to visit, and wanted to bring me a new voice student. I was so pleased to hear from her. The student she brought has great promise. And it's so nice to have another Ferrer in my life.

Geraldine Fitzgerald

My Irish angel first appeared in my life on a sound stage in Danbury, Connecticut, in 1967.

In March of '92, at a benefit for the Singers Forum, Geraldine gave a talk about that first meeting and this is what she said:

"...I would like to get on with telling you about how I first met Andy Anselmo, because I think it tells a great deal about him. It happened in Danbury, Connecticut, where there's a sound studio. Paul Newman and Joanne

Woodward and a very distinguished cast and myself were making a film called *Rachel, Rachel,* and the scene we were trying to shoot there was a scene where a crazy creature, played by myself, something on the order of Aimee Semple McPherson, was singing some crazy religious hymn to her congregation, and I was doing my best. Every time I sang my hymn, the sound man would start playing with his machinery and he'd start looking up and he would behave in this extraordinary way and we would complete the shot and he would come up to the director and he would whisper and point at me, saying things. After a very long time, it was decided we would dub it. Which you know is a really hateful thing to do, most of the time. And so I was very sad about that and we were breaking for the day and we were going back to New York, for we were all commuting. Among the people on the set was a young man called Andy Anselmo and he asked me if he could have a lift back to New York in the car that the studio provided. So I said, "By all means." And so he got in the car and we had a lot of talking together and I thought he was a most delightful person. And he said to me that he could help me with whatever I had to sing on the screen without causing catastrophe. I said I didn't think anybody could teach me to sing on any terms at all. He said, "I could. I could."

So when we said goodbye, I didn't really think we would ever meet again. But the next day, he telephoned me and said that someone who was coming to him for a lesson had failed to show up, and would I like to come over because he'd got some wonderful sugar cookies. And I said he was very charming. So I went over to his apartment. At that time I think he lived on 87th and Central Park West, wherever that is. And so he started to talk about singing and he said the audience didn't mind how narrow one's range was, that they didn't mind anything except the person not being involved with what they were singing. And he went on to say it was very much how actors feel about acting, that an audience doesn't mind what you're doing, as long as you're telling them the truth about your character, they don't really mind how you go about it. And so he said that on those grounds he would be able to teach me how to sing, no matter how short the range was. So with that in mind, I said that I would come. And one of the first things that he did for me was to stop me being afraid of making awful sounds and we used to accomplish that by doing exercises daily and telling me to sing them very, very loudly. So I sang them very, very loudly and from the cars in the street, people would point up at the window and they would stop dead. Anyway, we went on doing this and he always made me look at him when I was doing it because he wanted to stop me from being afraid from the first lesson. At this point, I would say that his genius as a teacher is to relax people from the fears they have gathered from their youth because many, many of us as youths, at school or in the choir or even going back to relatives in our lives who didn't like the way we sang, sort of put us off or made us nervous. And he says you are reborn with him in terms of being able to face the sounds or hear the sounds that you make and find them quite proper and find that they have a place in the world and that you should sing, we should all sing!

So this started really a whole chapter in my life that I never thought could possibly happen. I'd always wanted to sing but thought there was no way I could; but with Andy's teaching I now have a sort of singing act that still stays in perfect order and on the 4th of April I'm going to go out again, as I often do, and play it all around the country. I've even played the White House. And it's all entirely his doing. If I was to wish for something to happen to someone that I love, I'd wish that at some time in their life, they would be this lucky. I love Andy very much. I'm thrilled to be here."

It probably is gauche to print other people's compliments in your autobiography but her words reflect her spirit so perfectly that I just had to put them down for you.

My presence on that sound stage was actually the result of my lifelong adoration of Geraldine Fitzgerald, whom I had never met, and incredible luck. One of my students, Terry Kiser, was in *Rachel, Rachel,* his first real movie role. He had one fabulous scene, where he was the minister of some big church. It was very dramatic. I was teaching him and his girl friend, Beverly Hayes. They were both on soaps. I was teaching a lot of soap opera people at that time and I had gotten very friendly with those two; they were just great, two very talented people. We became close friends, so when Terry had to do this scene, he asked Beverly if she and I would be there while he was filming it, to give him support. Of course we would. And when he told me that Geraldine Fitzgerald was going to be there, I just flipped out. Because I was her Number One Fan, years before I ever met her! I used to go hear her lecture whenever she spoke. I remember one time she spoke at the HB Studios and her children were there. Oh, I was her best fan from the very beginning. When I saw her in *Dark Victory* and *Wuthering Heights* I was so moved by her beauty and her talent. I thought she was going to put Bette Davis off the map. That's what those two movies were: spectacular.

When Terry said that she would be there, I could not believe it. I thought, *I gotta go!* I told him how I felt about her, and then he told her what I said. By the time we met, she was all ready to meet me. In fact, they had a car for her and she didn't take it. (I know she forgot this part.) She came back in the car with us. The four of us talked along the way. She was so excited! I was, too. It was like two people who are meant to meet. And she wanted to learn to sing but no one, she said, would teach her. They said she didn't have any voice. They said forget about it. She said it was one of the big disappointments of her life. And I said, "Well, I know I can teach you. I've loved you for I don't know how many years and love can do anything." And she said, "I want to start immediately." So she did.

As she tells the story, she had only three notes to work with. She had smoked for many years, which made her voice very low. We started and she just listened to everything. She was excited about the whole process of it. She didn't care how she sounded. She didn't care for results. Nothing but the process mattered. She was the ideal student, a demanding thing for me. In one sense she was easy to teach, and in another, she wasn't. The fact that she was so famous put an extra burden on me, because I knew it was going to take time. People would hear her and if she didn't sound good, it would be my neck. Even so, it was a great time.

I learned so much from her! She had street smarts that I didn't have. She had a way of looking at things that was just brilliant. It was such a learning experience for me. We just learned from each other. It was the perfect combination. She came every day for years, and having her support and her interest in me and in my work, of course, was just a tremendous boost for my self-confidence. She kept saying, "You must do this. You must teach." I was not really ready to do it. I was just at the very beginning of my teaching, and I was on the fence about it. It was happening without my doing anything. Then she came along and made me feel how right it was, that I had the gift, that I had to share it. She made me feel all that. At times I thought, is she putting me on, or what? It was hard for me to understand why she was seeing me as a teacher. Not that she thought I shouldn't keep singing, she did. It took me a long time to come to grips with the fact that I was a teacher/performer, and not the other way round.

If she heard anybody or met anybody that she felt was really talented, she'd send them to me. She paid for their first lesson, to be sure they got to it. She called it their birthday present. That's how I had so many of the theater people coming to my studio. Mandy Patinkin, Mary Ann Plunkett, Geraldine Brooks, Dana Ivey—A whole slew of people. They, of course, talked to other people, and those people came, too. So it was a real turning point, meeting Geraldine Fitzgerald.

She had been around creative people with outstanding minds very early in life, like Orson Welles, who gave her her first break. That was her start in movies. And Charlie Chaplin, Henry Miller. She met those people, Laurence Olivier, Vivien Leigh. She learned a lot, fast, and she does have a grand mind. Even the dyslexia didn't interfere. She didn't even know she had it, for years.

We saw each other for many years, almost every day. I was very impressed because I was going through such a change in my life at that time, in relationships and in my career goals. She could read me like a book. She knew exactly if anything was wrong, the moment she walked into my apartment. It was amazing. I couldn't believe it. And she would call me every Sunday morning, to see how I was. I told her Sunday was my bad day. I'll never forget that. It went on for years. Her caring was so comforting.

She said I'd never be happy if I didn't take back my real name and sing lots of Italian music. So I became Andy Thomas Anselmo again, and resurrected my beloved Italian folk songs. Now I'm just Andy Anselmo, and I do it all and it's fine. I remember that I felt as a child that I didn't want to go through life as Santo (Italian for Saint) Anselmo. It just came back to me now!

I think this woman is one of those rare human beings, so spiritual and really caring, you know, everything a person should be, and yet she's simple. All that she has done and all the admiration and respect she has received, and all the money she's earned, and everything else, have absolutely not touched her. It's the way it should be, but so rarely is.

Geraldine is the force behind what I've done. She was the support, all those years. She was it. Her belief in me was so strong, in what I did and how I taught. She really brought the people to study with me, who went on and became famous, because she had a terrific eye for talent. I was very naïve then, as I look back at it. It wasn't until I healed myself when I met Geraldine that I began to mature, because she had those street smarts and I didn't and she was willing to share them. I never knew about those things. She taught me so much. That's why I feel the way I do about her. I knew what she gave me. I knew how much she believed in me and loved me, so I was able to trust her.

When you have a terrible experience, like the one I had with that one teacher, when I was about twenty-five, it stays with you and you think you'll never trust anyone again. You really think twice about everything that comes into your life. So maybe that's what the bad thing was for. It was for me to learn that. Otherwise, I wouldn't have known the difference.

Geraldine Fitzgerald is the Darlin' of my Heart!

Julie Harris

Charles Nelson Reilly brought Julie Harris to a rehearsal of the act he and I put together for my opening at the Bon Soir in New York. They were in *Skyscraper* together. Julie heard me sing for the first time that day. She said, "You sing the words like Frank Sinatra." If I hadn't been enchanted with her before she said that, I would have been enchanted with her afterward.

Then she came to take singing lessons from me. She sang a lot in *Skyscraper* and told me, "I need all the help I can get." She also came to my group classes at 73rd Street. She sat there quietly, taking it all in. I was thrilled. My students didn't know what a fantastic thing was happening to them. They were so self-involved, so fixed on what they personally would do in class, they didn't realize this great star was sitting there, learning with them.

Some time later, the Singers Forum was doing a presentation for Chase Manhattan Bank, in the art of personal communication and the uses of speech. It was a lunch-time show at the beautiful head office dining room. Some students sang. I spoke about our school. Julie then talked about the importance of art and quoted Emily Dickinson. Here we were in the temple of the money changers and she spoke magnificently about the need for art in all of life.

Julie came to my 70th birthday party and did part of Frankie's soliloquy from "Member of the Wedding." Then she sang "His Eye Is On The Sparrow" *a capella* and the crowd went wild.

Julie and I connect constantly. She's such fun, and so knowing about the theater and life itself. The Singers Forum and I owe her a great deal.

Maureen O'Sullivan

When I first met her, Maureen O'Sullivan had had seven children and looked about seventeen. She and Geraldine Fitzgerald had been friends for years. Geraldine wanted her to come and study with me. Eventually she came to my duplex on 87th Street for a class.

I was doing classes in different churches, little theaters and the Strasberg Institute. Geraldine and I were doing what we called "Street Theater" all around the city. I was teaching privately at home and had two evening classes every week. At first, Maureen came to those classes, and later took privately from me, too.

We worked on her favorite song, "Bewitched, Bothered and Bewildered," She sang it beautifully and, years later, she sang it in Woody Allen's movie, *Hannah And Her Sisters*. She gave a great performance and people in show business were amazed to find she had such a lovely voice.

Maureen told her daughter, Mia Farrow, about me. At one point, Mia was recording a children's album with songs and poems. I went to her apartment to help her sing it through. There were lots of interruptions and it wasn't the ideal way to work, but we did the best we could. I remember how pretty she looked, in a long, white dress. She seemed to be getting nervous and said she had to be through by five-thirty. I said we could stop any time. Then the bell rang and Woody Allen walked in, carrying a couple of bags of groceries. I looked at him and he looked straight through me. Mia didn't introduce us. I thought it strange behavior from one professional to another, but maybe it was the way he lived. Mia was such a nice, warm person. It wasn't her way, I was sure. I said to myself, "I've met more important people than Woody Allen," said goodbye to Mia, and left.

I remember one night, years ago, Maureen invited our little gang, Geraldine, John Harris and some other students and me to her apartment, so we could see her late husband, John Farrow's, Academy Award up close. It was sitting there on the mantel. The evening progressed from sincere admiration to wacky tributes to the statue itself, the Oscar as symbol, the speeches we would give if we won it. The speeches were absolutely hysterical and we decided we had to win an Oscar for the best acceptance speeches ever. They were all so funny. It's such a good memory.

A few years later, Maureen went on tour with a play and met James Cushing in Chicago. They clicked instantly and married soon thereafter. James was in the construction business and they had homes in New York, New Hampshire and Arizona. Whenever I went to visit my cousin, Arlene Ekin, and her family, in Arizona, I looked Maureen up and we would meet. The last time I saw her, Maureen, James, my cousin and her husband, Tom, my sister, Carolyn, John Harris and I had a wonderful lunch. I was host. Maureen looked so cute, wearing a baseball cap on her head. It looked great on her.

I knew she had lost some ground, physically. It was in her eyes. She seemed more dependent on James. I didn't think it was anything serious. We reminisced about Geraldine Fitzgerald. Maureen always wanted to know how the Singers Forum was doing and helped with donations over the years. She was good to us.

That last day, I wanted to get some pictures of all of us together. A couple were having lunch near us. I asked the man if he would take them for me. Tom said, "This is for Maureen O'Sullivan." The man said, "My wife will go bananas!" While he was taking pictures, he said to Maureen, "Just say it one more time, please." So she said it, backwards, "Me Tarzan, you Jane." We all laughed and then we all said goodbye.

When Maureen died, I sent Mia a note telling her how much her mother meant to me. I miss her as a presence in my life. She was a beautiful woman, unspoiled by her beauty and success. And so kind to me and my school.

Mandy Patinkin

As a birthday present to him, my Irish angel, Geraldine Fitzgerald, sent Mandy Patinkin to me. Geraldine had heard him singing in a car, going to New Haven. They were in a play, *Shadow Box,* that won a Pulitzer prize. She said, "You've got to do something with your voice. You have a voice there." He said, "No, I never want to study singing. I don't like teachers and I don't want to go to a teacher." She said, "Well, you should go to this man." And so she gave him me as a birthday present and he came and that was the beginning of it.

Not long ago, someone said that Mandy brought his special brand of insanity to *Chicago Hope.* Oh, well, one man's genius is another's insanity. When I first met him, he had that "insanity." He was so full of energy and off the wall he scared me, and that's not easy. He was unpredictable, except when he got down to work. I thought, if I can harness this genius, he will be a great singer. When he did the scales, this other person came through and that's when I realized who he really was, and what he really had to do. The way he worked was great: concentrating, giving himself to the work at hand, without editing, judging, any of that. I told him not to listen to himself or judge, just do it and we'd see where it's going to go. The singing, I think, has disciplined that "insanity" into something great, because that's what talent is: it's using whatever it is about you that's "off-the-wall" and making it work. I encourage that in all my students.

Mandy came to me when he was twenty-four. He was resisting singing. He considered himself an actor so he wasn't really motivated for singing. I always had to keep him doing it. I kept encouraging him, calling him to come for his lessons. I know there is a kind of self-destructive thing that some performers have. They seem to stop themselves from using all their talents. And, in a way, he was getting my attention.

Knowing that, I just kept trying to instill the idea that this is what he was going to do, that he had a very special quality and voice, and that people would absolutely love it and buy it. After a number of years, he bought it! I got his wife, Kathryn, to join me, because she knew he could sing. The wonderful thing about him was the fact that, no matter what, he really loved the exercises. He really loved the learning of the voice. He didn't want to sing a song. He didn't sing a song for a long time. We just worked on technique. We made tape after tape. I think he still has them all. He says he's got about a thousand of them, stored in banks all over the world. He was faithful in doing them. He enjoyed working with them every day. This is the kind of discipline he had when he got his first role in *Evita*. By then he had one song, and it was "Over The Rainbow." He sang it with his passion and gentleness and courage, at the audition.

Because of the way everyone reacted to his performance, I think it was the beginning of his believing that the voice would be a big part of his life. He sang magnificently, in a way that no one else had sung "Rainbow" before, much more expression of feelings, different dynamics and musicality in singing. It was a big, full sound, but what he did with it was his heart and soul. That's the part that more people seem to come for: soul. Now even the young people recognize it.

In January, '96, Mandy and Kathryn had invited me to brunch. He was coming in from the country and got slowed down by a snowstorm. It was wonderful because it gave me a chance to speak to Kathryn alone. There was about an hour that we had together, while Kathryn made coffee and fixed brunch for us. We rambled and we talked about things that we had noticed in Mandy's singing, and she was so happy I was there. She thought his breathing was getting a little off, and said his accompanist had mentioned it, too. I had noticed it myself. But it's very difficult, calling up somebody who's working every day and everybody tells him he's the greatest and you say, "Yeah, but you're not doing—this or that."

Finally Mandy came in. After brunch we went to a room that's his studio. We worked in there and we probably had the best session we've ever had. He was so open and free, and gave more of everything. I was able to say it straight, what I observed was going on, what I heard, how to take care of it. At the end of the lesson, he pulled out a book of arias that I had given him five years before. He said, "You know, I was thinking maybe it would be kind of fun if I threw an aria into the act." I said, "What? I can't believe what I'm hearing! Well, that would be just great."

So we turned to *La Boheme* and he sang "Che gelida manina."

Well, any tenor would give an eyetooth to sing it like he did. It was beautiful, so easy for him. He just floated up to those high notes. It was so moving to hear him sing it. I thought, *Oh, God!* I said, "You know, if you ever want to switch careers, boy, you could do it. An audience will go crazy over this." Then I said, "Really work on it and then we'll try to learn it." Then he left for Chicago.

Mandy and I work whenever he's in town. He works with the tapes constantly and it just makes all the difference in the world. That's what students don't know: you need the support of a teacher. That's what I love about Mandy. He didn't always understand that, but he understands it now and keeps this relationship going and knows that he should, knows the importance of relationships. He keeps his feet on the ground. I really think singing has a lot to do with it. Singing keeps you in a different place. Singing! (As opposed to shouting, belting, howling or even just acting.) Acting is always someone else's words and intent. The director is directing from word to word. It's been the death of more actors than I care to count. Singing is different.

Singing takes a self-awareness of some mighty proportions—not self-centered but self-aware—to know when you're doing it right and when you're not. It's like another lifetime. It's interesting how, as you live through it, it seems like different lifetimes. It's not all one. It's different stages and periods and it's very strong, very vivid at the time, and then you move out of that one into another one. They say cats have nine lives. I think singers do, too.

In June of '96, I got a call from Mandy, but he disguised his voice so well, I didn't know it was him. Then I recognized his laugh. He was so up, so happy. He said, "Everything is going along great. I'm with you every day."

He said he still vocalizes every day with our tapes. He had just come back from a concert in Cincinnati. He'd done seven concerts in London and they went fine. Then he did a movie there, and he and his family went to Greece for a month. He was back home but on Sunday he had to leave for Prague, to do *Hunchback of Notre Dame.* Then he'd be back in September and wanted to go back to work, singing. He said, "I've got to get back to it now." We talked about the Singers Forum. He sounded so good. He said they want him to do another record and he just hadn't had the time to get it together. Then he said, "I remember when I was dying to do a record and I never thought I'd get to do one. And now I'm putting them off! I was telling Kathryn this. It's so strange."

Sometimes Mandy holds his voice down, I think, too much. But when the need is there, he lets you know he has got this bigger voice.

In March of '97, there was a wonderful review in *Variety* of Mandy's benefit concert at the Lyceum Theater. They talked about his phenomenal range, what he does with his voice, what an entertainer he is. They said there is no one else around today who can do that, and that he's a throwback to Al Jolson, Judy Garland, all the great performers who could, solo, hold you for two hours. Then they said there is only one female performer who can do that today, and that's Liza Minnelli.

And she's my student, too.

I was so thrilled with it. I don't know of a teacher who has ever had the kind of students and performers I've had. I think it's exciting because these two people are beyond anybody out there today. There's no one else.

When I saw Mandy in Buffalo that same summer, I knew his performance had gone beyond everything he'd ever done. I spoke to him that week. He told me how well everything went, that he just couldn't thank me enough for making a suggestion about working with a microphone, that it would ease a lot of his problems, and working with the new exercises I gave him for what was happening to his voice had cleared everything up. It was all so warm and so loving. And he said, "We've got to get back to work now." He never said it quite like that before. He's reached another level of maturity. It's just the latest one. More to come.

Mandy and I have an ongoing relationship. We are friends, not just teacher and performer/student. We are truly family. I love him and his work and know his courage in adversity, his gratitude to those who have helped him through the hard times. There is no way to sum up Mandy Patinkin. His talents are boundless. His courage is unlimited. No teacher could have a more rewarding pupil.

Regis Philbin

Phyllis Diller and I were on tour. We had club dates all over the place and whenever she had publicity gigs scheduled on radio or TV, she brought me on. She was so generous about that.

This time we were in Los Angeles and we were doing an appearance on the *Regis Philbin Show* one afternoon. I remember I sang "Hello, Dolly" in Italian. It sounded very funny and I know Regis got a kick out of it. Phyllis was, as usual, very funny. She pretended never to have seen me before and said, "I went into the men's room accidentally and there he was!"

Then, years later in New York, Regis was doing an afternoon cable show. Saundra Santiago, the actress from

Miami Vice and *All My Children,* who studied voice with me, was booked for it. She really didn't know what to do as her "act" on his show. Then she said, "Why don't you come on and give me a singing lesson?" I saw Regis for the second time that day. He told me he was interested in singing and took part in the exercises I did with Saundra on the show.

About a week later, Regis called me. It was evening, about seven-thirty, and he said he had to go on stage and sing somewhere at eight. He asked, "What should I do?" I asked, "Why didn't you call me for a voice lesson today?" He said, "Please tell me what to do." I said, "Just breathe the way we did on your show." There was no time for anything more.

About a week later, Regis started lessons with me. He basically has a good tenor voice and we worked together for quite a while. At some point he told me that he'd made an album years before and it hadn't gone anywhere. It still bothered him and he always felt his voice wasn't "good enough" for a career. No matter how well he sang, and he was good, believe me, he just couldn't believe in his voice.

Regis brought me with him on several big shows. We'd do an Italian duet. I invited him to emcee at the Columbus Club when the Forum students did a show there. He invited me to go with him to clubs and we'd do our number. We were a big hit all over town.

Regis started doing the show with Kathy Lee about then. It took up more and more of his time. Everybody knows there is nothing in all show business more demanding than a live morning TV show. There's hardly room for anything else in your life.

After a while, we didn't hear Regis calling out, "Where's the coffee pot? Coffee, I want coffee!" as he always did when he came in the door. The receptionist put away the coffee pot and that was that.

Brooke Shields

Brooke Shields was sixteen when I met her. A lawyer, Richard Ticktin, called me one day to say he had a student for me, a young model, Brooke Shields. I said, "Oh, wonderful. I love Brooke Shields!"

She came with her mother to the Singers Forum, to study voice. I was so impressed with the love between Brooke and her mother, Terry. It was such a beautiful thing to see. Brooke was the sweetest girl you can imagine. She was beautiful outside and inside. She's stayed that way.

We started to work together. Her presence in the building caused people to follow her off the elevator and try to find her inside the Singers Forum offices. Terry suggested we put paper over the window into my studio. It worked for a while.

Brooke came to me whenever she was in town. We became good friends. We had photographers coming in and out of my studio all the time, doing publicity shots. We were in *The Star.* We were in *The Inquirer.* We were in all those supermarket rags. They loved her. It was very exciting and the school and I got fantastic publicity. I even got a call from *People Magazine* for an interview as part of their series on teachers. They never used it. Maybe they were hoping for a negative comment about Brooke or Terry, but they were knocking on the wrong door.

When Brooke decided to go to Princeton, Terry asked me to go out there to teach Brooke. We had to put paper on the windows there, too. Sometimes Terry would drive me out for a lesson, then we'd have lunch in town. I got to know her very well. Sadly, I couldn't keep going to Princeton. I had to cancel half a day's students, usually on short notice, and they were suffering.

From then on, whenever she was on a break from school, I would see her. One year, Princeton put on a musical and Brooke had a role in it. I went out with Terry to see the show and I was so proud of Brooke. Not only could she sing beautifully, but she could dance. She was wonderful. I said to her, "Brooke, you could really do a Broadway musical when you graduate from college!"

Brooke was still doing a lot of modeling. I didn't see her as much then but we always kept in touch through Terry.

One day, Terry called to say Brooke was doing a salute to Bob Hope at Radio City Music Hall. Terry wanted me to come and make sure Brooke was well-presented. Brooke was doing a musical number with Dorothy Lamour and other stars. I was to teach it to all of them. While I was doing that, Terry kept saying, *sotto voce,* "Give it to her. Take care of Brooke." Dorothy Lamour caught on and said, "Why is everything in her key? Why can't we do it in my key?" Big stars can be rather touchy. I said, "We'll find a key that suits everybody." I slanted it towards Brooke's key anyway. Bob Hope was so fond of Brooke. She absolutely loved him.

After Princeton, we had some lessons. She had a great birthday party on a yacht docked at the Water Club. Barbara Walters was there with her daughter. Big names and their kids were all over the place. It was not just a celebrity bash. Brooke's friends from home and school were there. I met her father and step-sisters. He was a very tall man, and very pleasant.

102

When she did *Grease* she was very good. It opened up theater and television to her. It was a wonderful career move. I remember I brought her a Singers Forum baseball cap to wear on stage. We had a great time. Then Brooke said, "I want you to meet someone." It was Andre Agassi. I almost didn't recognize him. He looked so mature, all the long hair cut off. The rapport, the affection they had for each other was heartwarming. She was so happy and I was happy for her.

One night there was a party at Liza Minnelli's. I walked in late and there was Brooke. We hadn't seen each other for a while and Brooke was so dear. She asked, "What would you like to eat? I'll fix it for you." She took such good care of me. We had a long talk. She was an adorable, sweet girl and still is.

Once Terry called and asked me to come to Hollywood. Brooke was starring in *Sahara,* a movie Terry was producing. Terry wanted Brooke to sing over the title. Brooke wasn't really comfortable with that idea. I stayed at a fabulous hotel for about three days. We worked on a big M-G-M sound stage. It was a dream come true. I was on the M-G-M lot at last, and performing, in a way. It was so exciting. We worked on separate sound tracks, I think, so I could sing the song, phrasing it as I thought she would, and she would sing on her track. I thought it came out pretty well, but Brooke wasn't happy with it and in the end it wasn't used. The script called for Brooke to play a boy. Can you picture Brooke Shields as a boy? That's Hollywood.

Brooke has such presence, such beauty, such intelligence, I'm sure people envy her desperately. She's also had to be a strong person. She's had to take charge of her life. She's had to go through divorce. She's had to endure the sudden loss of a much loved co-star.

In case you didn't know, fame, fortune, and beauty are no protections against harsh reality.

Liza Minnelli and Billy Stritch

The thing about Billy Stritch was that he had never studied singing. I was reading *Backstage* and there was an article on new performers. Billy was in it and he was quoted about his career. He said he had never studied singing but was interested in doing it. So when I read that, I went to the telephone and called him. I knew that he was Liza Minnelli's music arranger. We spoke and I invited him to have a lesson at the Singers Forum. I could tell that he'd be wonderful to teach because he was so open and there wasn't an ego in the way. I could tell what I could do with his voice because it was not messed up by anything. He needed to strengthen it and find his own unique quality with it. So we started. Now it's been eight years and I really can't believe it's been that long. It doesn't seem so to me. Of course, we haven't worked every week. He goes out on the road a lot, but he always comes back, so there is always continuity. That's the most important thing in singing lessons. The way his voice has developed, as I can tell from hearing the tapes during these years, is just great.

After about six months, Billy told me Liza Minnelli had heard him sing and she was so excited about his voice. I don't know if he had told her he was studying. She just couldn't believe what had happened to his voice over time. He told her about me and she said, "I've gotta go over there and study with that man."

Billy's travel schedule is dizzying but he calls a lot. I do see him whenever he's performing in my neighborhood. A particular summer night in Connecticut comes to mind. It's really all about the *bel canto* technique and what happens if you learn it and use it.

When you're young, you can play around with your voice as if it will never go away. The idea of studying or taking care of it never seems to enter your mind. Lessons with a good teacher can teach you how to take care of your voice so that it can grow and last. You don't realize that when you're young and you have that youth on your side. To me it's very boring to go to clubs and have to hear people performing who feel they don't need to study, that if they study, they'll lose this fantastic, unique, natural quality that makes them a cabaret singer. They don't even know what a cabaret singer is. It's all a muddle. Where this all started, I don't know, but it's bad, because young people are not developing their voices. It was so obvious that night in Connecticut, when Billy sang. He had this really beautiful sound and he was still a cabaret singer. He was putting out what he wanted to and he was getting off what he wanted to. It was all a beautiful sound. Some singers don't pay attention to sound. They get indulgent with the lyrics so the lyrics don't get active. They think that if they go on and pull their voices in and pull themselves in, that is acting. It is not acting, nor is it singing.

This particular night, a man was on the bill and a young girl. They shall be nameless, out of the goodness of my heart, though the girl singer had great potential. The man seemed to have this idea that you get up on the stage and it just happens. Out steps the little secretary and sings and dances her way into saving the show. Or the mail room clerk. Just like in *Forty-Second Street*. I was amazed. That's still going on. With even a knowledgeable man like that, it can happen. He never came out of his dressing room after the show. I never did see him. But I did speak to Billy, of course, and told him he sang beautifully even with a sound system that wasn't very good. And even though there was a bat, flying around the people on stage all evening, and around the tops of our heads. This was a star-struck bat, a theater bat. Summer theater is like that sometimes: weird.

Now Billy and I work together whenever he's in town. He is all music, from head to toe.

Liza Minnelli remembered that I was in an acting class with her at HB Studios before she did *Flora, the Red Menace.* She must have been very shy because she sat way in the back of the class and never said a single word. She was gorgeous. At the end of the semester, we all had to do a number or a soliloquy or whatever. Liza came forward in that class and bowled us all over like ten-pins. She had absorbed every word, every nuance, every suggestion made by the teacher, Charles Nelson Reilly, incorporated them into her performing soul and left us standing in her dust. It was a revelation to me, and I never forgot it.

Liza did call me and we went to work as soon and as often as she could. When she was in town, she liked to start work about four-thirty P.M. She sent her car for me because there was no way I could get to her apartment by cab then. It was a special time for me and our hours together over the years are dear to me.

In September, '95, Billy and Liza called me from Bally's in Atlantic City. They told me the tour was going great and Billy was warming himself and Liza up before every performance and before working on the tapes for a new recording. They were going to Nashville for a day or two to do something there with the tapes and then they were leaving for South America. They were so excited about it all. They said they'd be back by the middle of October.

Billy was just so appreciative, so warm, with me. There's a difference in the tone of his voice to me. He is grateful for what I've helped him do. When you work with someone, you hear the voice developing. You see what's coming, what it's doing to your student. It really gives you a greater understanding of what the technique does. He sounded really wonderful, and then, at the end, he said that he loved me. I was so moved. I think he's the coming male triple threat, vocally, musically and as a personality.

It's just great that Liza has him, because he is so stable. He can help her with everything. I'm always anxious to hear what his voice is like when he comes back. It keeps growing. I decided to give Billy the first annual Andy Anselmo Achievement Award and it was a big night at the National Arts Club.

Liza's work schedule is amazing. She flies from continent to continent, city to city, hotel to hotel. She's endured terrible pain, had several operations and gone through emotional trauma during the years I've known her.

Let me tell you about the night I went with two of my students, Jerry and Peggy King, to see Liza at Foxwoods, the Connecticut casino. The weather was frightful. We left a tornado in our wake and blinding rain held us up, but we made it in time for her show at nine o'clock. Liza sang gorgeously. Her voice was clear and strong. When she sang softly, it was so pretty. She sang "Embraceable You" and she told me later that she knew I was out there. And she sounded great. She was thinking about her technique. She sat on a stool with just piano accompaniment, and she sang the song because we had been working on that soft, higher voice for so long and she wanted to do it right, up there on the stage. Then she thought of her father, Vincent, and she got very emotional. She was afraid she couldn't continue with the song, but she did and those feelings were so strong, so moving.

That's how songs work. You start with an idea and you don't know where it's going to take you. You have to just go with it while you're singing it. The song becomes a much stronger experience, not only for the performer but for the audience.

After the show, her secretary came out and took us backstage. Liza's dressing room door was closed. Billy came in. Then Liza appeared and said she was so hot from the show she had to shower and wash her hair. We had seen the sweat flying from her during the performance.

Liza said she'd been practicing. She just seemed like her old self. She said she wanted to do a lot of work when she next got a chunk of time in New York. When she met Peggy and Jerry, she said to me, "You're surrounded by your students." She sat next to Peggy and I thought Peggy would faint.

In June, '96, Liza did a show with Regis Philbin and Kathy Lee. In the studio audience was a young woman made up to look exactly like Liza: hair, makeup, black dress, everything. It was spooky. There are always several of these ladies around whenever Liza performs. To me, this kind of imitation is not the sincerest form of flattery. Flowers and a nice note would be better.

A career like Liza's is not easy. There are too many distractions, too many pressures. When you're that famous, the pressure of having to be great all the time is tremendous. You can't go out in public on your own. The bigger you are, the worse it gets. I saw it when Madonna came backstage at Carnegie Hall to see Liza. The way her bodyguards maneuvered her in and out of the place was the most amazing thing. She always has to be surrounded by four or five bodyguards. They protect her and squire her away before the fans know what's going on. When Madonna got up to where Liza was, I had the opportunity to speak to her and to this day I regret I didn't. I didn't know quite how to handle it without appearing pushy. There was the moment, but I didn't know how to take it. I guess it's hard for a Sicilian Catholic to say, "Hello, Madonna! How are you?" Madonna means only one thing to us, the Mother of Christ. I really just wanted to say, "I'm Liza's teacher," and talk a little bit about singing and her voice. I know *bel canto* technique helps all singers. I didn't quite know how to handle it. "Hi, Madonna, let me fix your voice," was not the way to go.

Liza has to have bodyguards, too. I got caught up in it once. I didn't know what was happening. All of a sudden I found myself being swept into a limo. I said, "Where are we going? What's happening?" I wasn't prepared. Nobody warned me. Talk about fast! I think performers enjoy it sometimes, but it depends on the tenor of the crowd.

Several years ago, Liza was doing Carnegie Hall with Charles Aznavour and they were there for two weeks. I'd been working with her for months before that and things had really started to change. Now she wanted me to come backstage and warm her up every night. I'd get there at six o'clock and it was such a happy time. She was very close to Charles Aznavour. She loved having me come and warm her up and we were like a family. We had a wonderful time. She had the conductor's dressing room. There was an ante-room where her guests could come, and a big table was set up with food and drinks. After the show on opening night, people like Donna Karan and Michael Feinstein and I forget who else, were there, all people Liza feels close to. So they said, "Well, Liza?" I was there and I heard them. They said, "Liza, what has happened to your voice? You sound great! What happened?" Everybody was saying it. Finally she said, "You've all been asking me what's been happening to my voice. I want you to meet the man who's responsible for the change, Andy Anselmo." Everybody applauded. It was so unexpected. Praise, indeed.

I got friendly with Charles Aznavour. I even asked him if he would do a master class for the Singers Forum. He was the one who kept telling Liza, "You've got to work on your voice. You have got to." He was glad to meet me. He said that he doesn't do any studying now, that he has a few scales he does to warm up, but he knows the importance of study in keeping up your voice, especially as you get older. He's up there in his seventies, too.

That was opening night. The New York papers mentioned the change in Liza's voice. I came in the next evening with the reviews. I said, "Liza, have you read your reviews?" She said, "Oh, read them to me!" I said, "They all talk about your voice. They all noticed the change. Isn't this exciting?" I read them to her while she was making up. They said things about her new "pop-operatic" voice. I said, "Don't you love these words?"

It was a wonderful two weeks. Then I had pictures taken with her. They're on my wall in my studio at the Singers Forum.

In March, '97, Liza called and asked me to come over and have dinner with her and just talk. She had been through her hip operation and a throat operation and she wanted to begin again. Now that her voice was totally rested, she felt that she could start working on her technique and getting her voice going again. She had performances coming up and now her sound was like a young girl's voice, higher than before. Her speaking voice had such a wonderful, healthy lilt to it. I couldn't wait to see what a couple of exercises would do.

We went to the piano and started, and I gave her the bending over exercise, where it's impossible to control your voice. You stand, feet apart and parallel, bend over as far as you can and let your head hang down loosely. You just have to let the voice do what it's going to do on its own. And you feel yourself breathing, really breathing, all the way to your back. Next you sing a middle C octave, breathing in and singing EE OH NO on each note. When Liza did that, a voice came out of her that I had never heard. I've always loved her voice but this was another voice to love. It was healthy, with a beautiful, smooth quality to it. It was startling, as if a totally different person was singing. She couldn't quite believe that this was really happening. There was one octave that was totally clear and her vocal cords were meeting and functioning perfectly. It was just like starting over. Going up the octave and then down, the new voice was still not quite ready to fall into place. That was going to take a little while.

When Liza did *Victor-Victoria* there had been a crackling sound that usually happens after a period of abusing your voice, but it was gone now. That was a very difficult role. To lower the speaking voice, to sound like a man, really put a lot of heavy pressure on it. There was a lot of damage done by that role. She's been working very hard for a great many years and the voice finally said, "I want a rest." It was the best thing, Liza said, that ever happened, even though it was difficult and traumatic. When you're resting your voice, you wonder if it's ever going to come back. But what a revelation that first lesson was!

It was very tricky because I had to be careful of what

we did and not do too much. I wanted her to tell me how it felt the next day but I didn't hear from her. I had the feeling that it may not have felt as good as it would feel the next day. It would skip a day. But when we worked, it was very exciting to hear. She made the sound and it was like working with a new student who was just starting to train.

Many working professionals have this kind of trouble but they don't allow themselves time to recover. Their agents are booking them seven years ahead. That's what keeps causing them problems. The voice gets no rest.

Coming back after a throat operation, slowly working the voice back is a very traumatic thing because if anything's wrong with your throat and you're a singer, you think, *My God, it's never going to come back!* after every cold, every laryngitis. It was really rough going because Liza was operated on for polyps. I know that they had to clean out a lot of gunk (surgery isn't my specialty) but I saw the "after" pictures of her throat and it was totally clear. It was great. Her voice went up now that her throat was clear. It meant working it differently and getting her used to the new feeling. It's a different feeling from when you're pushing your voice down there in the belt voice. You're getting out this larger range. A new, lovely sound came from her. It was just thrilling. Then she started to feel better about her gorgeous new sound. At first she didn't know what to make of it. So then we started to expand from the top of the octave to the bottom. The rough part was at the bottom, where she speaks, and where the damage had been done in the low voice. That will take time. But the top was coming and we went up to Gs and A-flats. It was amazing because I had not been able to get that before. That's what made all the difference, recovering the ease and the smoothness. Then one day her accompanist came and he was floored by the whole thing, pleased but a little bit stunned that he had to raise Liza's keys. He wasn't prepared for that. He didn't know what the arrangers would say. All the arrangements would have to be changed. But he was excited about it, too. He just loved it. We were able to see what happened with her songs. It was wonderful, the freedom and the nuances and different kinds of musical phrasing that came out of Liza. She was having a really good time.

Then we had a big, general rehearsal with the boys who are backing her, singing with her. Three boys, the director and the pianist were all there. They hadn't heard her and when they heard this voice, everybody was stunned. I mean they went through the gamut of emotions, stunned, excited and then thrilled. When they tried a musical number together with the boys, the blend was beautiful and exciting. All of them were blending better with Liza. That was terrific.

They were supposed to go to Palm Beach for two concerts, one show a night, but then those shows had to be cancelled. A bruise on Liza's left leg was acting really badly and the doctors were afraid to let it go any longer. So they had to take her to the hospital for treatment. Everything was fine after that. It gave her more time to rest her voice.

To have her voice turn out like that was fabulous. I think she got happy and comfortable with it. She was saying, "I don't know who I am because it feels so different." And I was saying. "Well, it's still you but it's freer, more relaxed."

Oh, there's nothing like *that* ease in singing and feeling confident that your voice will do what you want it to do! I believe the only way that can happen is through the *bel canto* technique that shows you how to have that ease. Many singers don't know it exists. And it's the only way that's fun. Otherwise, no matter how much money you're making, singing can be pretty painful. You never feel right about it, or enjoy it, really.

The first days of October, '97, were very exciting for me because one Sunday night we had the Faculty Follies at the Singers Forum in New York. I performed better than I had in years. My voice was back and I was in great shape. Liza came with a friend who's involved in raising money for AIDS causes, Liza's big charity interest. Her presence really made the occasion very exciting for the cast and everybody was psyched from it. I have to say I was a very funny master of ceremonies. I was turned on because Liza was there. It was fun. At the end, I said, "A wonderful thing happened tonight. Sitting in this very room, in this very space, is the world's greatest entertainer, Liza Minnelli." The audience didn't know she was there. The place went crazy when she stood up. She stood up several times during the show. She gave me a standing ovation, and John Harris, too. I never heard applause from eighty people like I heard that night.

Liza said, "I just want to say something. This man has helped to restore my voice. I have had a terrible time. I had an operation on my throat. I went back to singing too soon. It did not help. And it's been just a terrible time. But—" And then she gave me such accolades about what I had done for her voice. The next day I went over to work with her. She had heard the sounds from everybody in that concert that I wanted her to make. She really picked up on it, just the way she did at the acting class when she was a teenager. She understood something she hadn't understood before. We had the most fantastic lesson. Her whole voice fell right into place. It was beautiful. It's very different. You know it's her. The sound is rich and smooth and full. We were jumping up and down for joy after every exercise. We couldn't believe what was happening. She got on the phone and called I don't know how many people and sang to them. She said, "Listen. Listen to what I can do!" She sang "Cry Me A River." It was beautiful. Everyone was just amazed.

I got her working with the microphone and really got that down so she can let the mike do the work for her instead of feeling she has to do it all. She fell in love with our guitarist. He is marvelous, teaches and plays for our jazz class. And she said, "Do you think he'd come and I could just sing quietly with him?" I said, "Oh, he'd love it." So when I told him, he was absolutely thrilled. She called her staff in to hear her sing the songs she'd be doing. Everybody came in. She said, "You know, Andy, these people have been through it all with me."

Later, I saw Billy and heard his new CD and said to him, "Billy, all those singing lessons must have paid off." It's a whole different sound, so lush, so musical, so pretty, so warm. He did all Brazilian songs. It's Louisa Schiff's record company and they did a big kickoff with it. They really did it right.

Liza was talking about doing an album that Billy will put together.

During all this, my sister, Annetta, was having operations for her hip and knee problems. Liza knows a lot about it because of her own hip and knee problems. Annetta was very depressed. I thought that speaking to Liza might pick her up, so I asked Liza and she said, "Of course. I know all about hips and knees and depressions." She was wonderful with Annetta. She said, "I heard you have a fella. That's great. That's more than any of us here have." She said, "Well, it just takes time." Then she said,

"I have to have a knee operation, too." She really said wonderful things to my sister and Annetta did cheer up after that. Liza was able to focus like that and help a woman she's never met, in the midst of her own struggles.

So now you know my friends Liza and Billy as I know them. Being a star is not all a one-way trip to Paradise. But Liza and Billy are passionate about their art and that's what it takes: passion.

Joanne Woodward

On June 15, 1995, when I began this book, the first thing I recalled was something Joanne Woodward told me, early in our friendship. It meant a lot to me then and it means even more now. She spoke of the Academy Award she won for her role in *Three Faces of Eve.* That night, after the presentation, the applause, the congratulations, the parties, she and Paul Newman returned to their hotel room. She sat, exhausted, looking at the Oscar and finally said to Paul, "Is that all there is to winning an Oscar?" and he said, "Yes. Get used to it."

You'd think winning the Oscar for Best Actress would have been a lifelong boost to her ego, if not to her bank account. Paul was saying it's not. It's only a brief, flashing moment, a decoration to be set on the mantelpiece and endlessly dusted.

I first met Joanne and Paul on the set of *Rachel, Rachel.* She was starring and Paul was directing. A student of mine, Terry Kiser, and his girl friend, Beverly Hayes, asked me to be on the set for Terry's big scene as the minister and told me Geraldine Fitzgerald would be in that scene, too. Nothing on God's green earth would have kept me from that movie set.

It was a fabulous day. Joanne and Paul were cordial to Beverly and me. Terry's scene was a great success. Geraldine and I began our loving connection that same day. Who could ask for anything more?

A couple of years later, Michael Cristofer, another student of mine and a Pulitzer Prize-winning playwright, was directing Joanne in an off-Broadway revival of Shaw's *Candide*. He suggested she work with me on her speaking voice for the stage, especially on her breathing and projection. That was the beginning of a very happy association. I went to many rehearsals and worked with Joanne every day. I gave her some singing exercises to strengthen the voice and in the process, discovered she had a beautiful sound.

When the play closed, Joanne started taking singing lessons from me a couple of times a week and developed a real singing voice. We had a great time. Paul loved to hear her sing. She sounded so good, a record producer asked her to do a song and a duet with me on an album he was making, called *Jerome Kern Revisited, Vol. IV.*

Then Joanne's young daughter, Melissa, who had the potential for a beautiful operatic voice, began to study with me. In time, the sound was glorious, angelic. At the same time, I was training the voices of the three principals of *Agnes of God*: Geraldine Page, Amanda Plummer and Lee Remick, during rehearsals. When the producers looked for a voice to be heard as the young nun, Agnes, I recommended Melissa and the producers went wild over her voice. For some reason, she didn't feel she wanted to do the role. I was disappointed and so was Joanne, but she was wise enough not to push Melissa.

Joanne and Melissa began to attend the performing classes I held at the Singers Forum several times a week.

Paul would come early to watch them perform and take them home. The Forum students would go into silent ecstasies, but obeyed our rule: no screaming, no fainting, no requests for autographs or lifetime contracts, no matter who comes into the school. I know it was difficult for them, but they made it.

I especially remember Joanne and Paul inviting me to see the inimitable, irrepressible Bobby Short at the Carlyle Hotel. Paul barely glanced at Bobby. He never took his eyes off Joanne.

Joanne appeared at my 70th birthday party and benefit for the Singers Forum at the Roundabout Theater, and she was great.

I was always a bit intimidated by Paul. He has the ability to focus in a way that blocks out intrusive and multitudinous fans. A friend of mine once saw him waiting for his family just inside a Chinese restaurant off Lexington Avenue, and said he was relaxed but unapproachable, like the Michelangelo "David," looking off into the distance. That's a necessary talent for any performer of Paul's magnitude and it must save him endless trouble.

Paul and Joanne are the most romantic couple I've ever known, in or out of the profession. I am happy to have them in my world.

My dear parents, Loretta and Angelo Anselmo.

The act Tom, Dick and Carrie—two guys and a doll. Actually, the beautiful Rita Noble, Johnny King, my oldest friend, and me in New Orleans touring the best hotels in the U.S., booked by the largest agency at the time, M.C.A. of America.

Where my school really began—the apartment on 73rd Street and Riverside Drive. Who would have dreamed this would all happen!

The so very gifted Robert Morse, star of Broadway, TV and movies, one of my earliest friends and supporters.

Charles Nelson Reilly, the funniest man in the world. Gifted actor, teacher and director, my greatest supporter.

Composer—Pulitzer Prize winner for best musical, *The Golden Apple*—Jerome Moross.

Rod McKuen—I was a fan.

Chairman of our Board and special friend, Louis Tallarini (left)
with, of course, Luciano Pavarotti and yours truly.
(*Photo courtesy of Allen Rokach*)

The great opera star Marilyn Horne, and me.

Mandy Patinkin, who studied with me starting at age 23. We worked a long time and to this day we are still close friends. Mandy has a big heart. He is always there to help our school, The Singers Forum. The *New York Times* calls him "The greatest performer of our time." I love him.

One of my many orchestra performances in New York and around the country.

Opening night of *Phantom of the Opera* with my sisters Carolyn and Annetta Priore, my dear friends Frances Levine, Rosemary Hayes, John Harris, and our congenial driver.

My two sisters whom I've always adored—Carolyn and Annetta.

A great friend. Maxine Andrews of the Andrews sisters, one of our students and supporters.

The extraordinary actress and recipient of dozens of awards, Julie Harris—one of my great supporters.

My great sudent, Geraldine Fitzgerald, award-winning actress from stage and screen—my mentor and friend.

Philip Campanella and I with my student and great performer, Eartha Kitt.

A special award from Canisius College in Buffalo, New York, from the president, Vincent Cooke S.J.

The Big Three of the Singers Forum—Philip Campanella joined us and saved our lives—Philip, John, and me.

The love of my life, 11-year-old Caroline Jones, a very gifted singer and songwriter whose voice will thrill the world—with her mother, the dynamic Sonja.

Paul Tudor Jones, my mentor, my friend and benefactor.

My beautiful home in Chautauqua County. Originally my
grandfather's grape farm—104 years old.

Billy Stritch and Liza Minnelli, the greatest entertainer of them all, and me after one of my concerts.

My 70th birthday benefit at the Roundabout Theatre. Flanked by a great array of stars, mostly students. Liza Minnelli, Billy Stritch, Portia Nelson, John Harris, Geraldine Fitzgerald, Mandy Patinkin, Joanne Woodward, Jerry Stiller, Julie Harris, Anne Meara.

Great Ladies

Lucine Amara

While a student at the New England Conservatory of Music in Boston, I used visualization in a special way to get me through the hard times. When I felt poor, when I didn't have any money, maybe just a little change in my pockets, I would walk through the Ritz Carlton or the Copley Plaza hotels and sit in the lobby for a while, watching the people who could afford to stay there, as they passed. Then I'd go into the coffee shop and sit at the counter and have coffee.

One Sunday, I chose the Copley. I was to be paid the next day, but that day I had hardly anything. I sat at the counter and ordered coffee. There was only one other person in the place, a striking woman with an air about her. Over the loudspeaker came a voice saying, "Telephone for Lucine Amara," and the woman said, "Oh, that's me," got up and left. I thought, *Lucine Amara! She's singing with the Metropolitan Opera company here in Boston!*

When she came back, I got up my courage and spoke to her. I said, "Are you here with the Met?" She said, "Yes, I'm singing with the company." We began to have a nice conversation. I told her that I was a voice student. She said, "I know you can't afford to buy a ticket, but would you like to come as my guest tonight?" I'll never forget that. I said, "Oh, that would be great!"

She got me in to see *Marriage of Figaro*. I went backstage to thank her. She had a lovely voice. She was such a nice, down-to-earth kind of person. She was not a diva-diva-diva. I asked if she would like to come see the Conservatory. I would give her the tour. I told her about Mr. Whitney, my great teacher, and said I would show her his room. She did come and we had fun. We were contemporaries and shared the same passion for music and the voice. Over the years we kept in touch. When I finally moved to New York, I called her. She actually lived only a block away from me on 73rd Street. I took her to parties. Sometimes she would call me and I would go to see her do something at the gorgeous old Met.

One night I couldn't get there till about a quarter to eight and she had me meet her at the stage door. She was doing the Countess in *Marriage of Figaro* and she came from her dressing room to the stage door with my ticket, in full costume and makeup. I couldn't believe she had that kind of concentration! She was so cool about it all. That was the kind of relationship we had, and off and on, we'd call each other just to say hello, or we'd meet somewhere for coffee and talk.

In 1997, Anita Darian, a wonderful singer who has done a lot of fine things, gave a benefit program at the Singers Forum and invited Lucine, who is a very close friend of hers. I was out of town. By this time, Lucine had retired from the Met. When she discovered that this was my school, she just couldn't get over it. She was floored by the whole thing. I called her to say I was sorry to miss her visit, but glad she liked the school.

While she was there, a student, Denise Galon, met her and told her she was doing *Aida* with another student, Liz Russo, and asked if it would be possible for

Mme. Amara to coach them in the two leading roles. Lucine was amenable and a little time went by. Then Denise won first prize in a competition at Carnegie Hall and Liz took second prize. This is almost unheard of in contests at this level, but they were simply superb that night. Denise was so excited, she called Lucine and asked if they could work on *Aida* now. Lucine said, "Yes!" In June of '98, she came to the school and worked on *Aida* for several hours with Denise and Liz. She would not charge them. I again had a prior unbreakable commitment but John Harris was there. They all had the most fantastic time. What a way to learn at first hand! Lucine was one of our great Aidas. She did it in Italy, at the Caracalla, she did it at the Met. I saw her do it many times. Denise and Liz worked like real pros.

How often do students have the privilege of working so closely with a big star from the Met? It doesn't just happen. It's difficult for young students to understand about long-term relationships. Whatever it is, it never seems to go away. There is a bond I seem to establish with people. I do work at relationships with people I love and respect, and I have them to pull out at times like this. That's why this incredible experience happened to Denise and Liz. Lucine came back at the end of August to do the parts they didn't get to in June. She wants to do both roles with them. She's just amazing.

More recently, I invited Lucine to do a master class at Singers Forum. She is a brilliant teacher and helped each student in expert fashion. I was there for that one and I was as excited as the students by her wisdom and caring. We'll get together again soon and have coffee (decaf, now) and talk up a storm. Now I can treat her to coffee.

Ingrid Bergman

My only encounter with Ingrid Bergman was brief but memorable (to me!). I had taken my mother to see one of my dearest friends and students, Maureen O'Sullivan, in a Broadway play, *Morning's at Seven.* I had my camera with me to take a picture of us with Maureen and whoever else might come backstage.

Soon after the show, when we were in Maureen's dressing room, who should appear briefly in the doorway but Ingrid Bergman! She was a tall, elegant woman and I was so taken aback that by the time I remembered the camera, she had disappeared. I haven't forgiven myself yet.

Many years earlier, I was doing my inspirational singing program at St. Peter's Church in New York City. Somehow it had caught on. The word spread all over town. There were two shows every day. One morning when I arrived, the church was full of TV cameras and technicians milling about. They were there to tape me for the six o'clock news. The reporter who interviewed me was Pia Lindstrom, Ingrid Bergman's daughter.

Many years later, at a benefit to raise money for the Suicide Foundation, I was seated next to Isabella Rossellini, again (Ingrid Bergman's daughter).

The world is really a very small place. Uncanny, how it goes round and round and the same people keep reappearing. (Or at least their progeny!)

Phyllis Diller

One day I read in the trade paper, *Show Business,* that Phyllis Diller was coming to town, to cast for a summer

TV series to be done in New York. So I told Charles Nelson Reilly, with whom I was studying, about it and said, "I have to do this. I want to do this. I want to meet Phyllis Diller. I want to sing for her because I know I'll get that show."

Charlie made the phone call to the producer. I'm not sure if the producer arranged it or if Charlie got to Phyllis Diller herself. She was appearing at the Americana Hotel, now the Sheraton. When I went there, Charlie came with me. The producer was there, too. Phyllis came in. I was floored by her, because she was not at all flashy. She didn't have the wigs and the whole wild persona. She was so quiet. We had the audition right there. She asked me if I would like to sing. I forget now what I did sing, but she was the best audience I've ever had. She sat there, totally involved, took in everything, totally quiet, totally still. I was so impressed. She never drew attention to herself. I know I did sing well. I was inspired by her. She said, "You're a male Barbra Streisand. You sing the words like Barbra!" Barbra was real hot. I couldn't have asked for a better compliment than that. Phyllis said, "Are you available to do the show?" I said I would make myself available, that I would just love to work with her. It was that easy. I got the job.

We've been friends ever since. In 1994, she introduced me at my 70th birthday party at the Roundabout Theater in Manhattan. She opened the show. She couldn't be there so her voice came out on tape and it was hysterical.

She was another one of the people I've met who followed a way of thinking, a philosophy, metaphysics, visualization, spiritual commitment, whatever you want to call it. It's a creative process. They all have a positive approach to life. She was the most positive of all.

After the summer, we went on tour. I became her protégé. I played a lot of places with her. I got to know her very well and we had many late night discussions about her philosophy and positive thinking. She carried around a carton of books with her, to hand out to people. The book was *The Magic of Believing,* by Bristow, a Pocket Book edition. Whenever anyone asked, "How can I break into show business?" she would go to the carton and take out a book and say, "Read this book. This book changed my life."

She tells the story of always having to be the breadwinner. Her first husband, she thought, was very rich, but it turned out he wasn't and he couldn't hold on to a job. She always had to work. She got a job selling in a department store in San Francisco. One day, the manager came around to all the salespeople and said, "Look, we've got to do something to pick up sales. They're really dropping. I want you all to read this book." He passed out copies of *The Magic of Believing.* She went home and read it, came back the next day and said, "I read this book all night. It says that I can be anything I want to be. And I want to be the funniest woman in the world and I'm going to start right now. So I quit." And she did.

She started that day putting an act together for herself. In the beginning it was a singing act. She sang funny songs. She had studied singing at a conservatory in Ohio. She liked singers and singing. In nine months, she had her first engagement in San Francisco, at the Purple Onion. She said they hired her because they felt sorry for her. She was in her late forties by that time and she looked like everybody's mother. She said they seemed to be thinking, "What is this woman doing in show business?" But they liked her and she started with the singing act.

And it was this act that I saw in New York at Number One Fifth Avenue. She played there and I remember one of the numbers where she was sitting on the piano, lying all over it, and I thought it was a really bad act. Finally she realized she had to talk if she was going to make it. She dropped the singing and spoke. She said the first time she did it, she didn't know how she lived through it. It was that frightening. She said it was the most difficult thing she ever did in her life.

I can never say enough about Phyllis Diller. She was like Geraldine Fitzgerald to me. These two women were just extraordinary to me. They helped me so much. Phyllis brought me on all the talk shows, all the TV shows she did. She would tell them, "I want him to sing on the show." You have that power when you're in her position. I did so many wonderful shows with her.

Once we were booked into the Shoreham Hotel in Washington, D.C. We arrived there in the afternoon. We were going to rehearse and then we'd do our show. I was first on the bill. It was to be in what they called the Terrace Room, a beautiful outdoor space. It was summertime. We arrived in the lobby of the hotel and it was packed with people. I said, "Phyllis, this is weird. All these people and there's not a sound." She said, "I think they're deaf and dumb." (These days we say "hearing impaired, speech impaired," but way back then no one thought anything of using those unkind words.) I said, "What kind of an audience are we going to have tonight?" She said, "How about that?"

I'll never forget that opening night. We had rehearsed in a big room where they had the shows during the winter. The band was fabulous. I was looking forward to opening the show. I never thought of doing a sound check outside. I don't know why because I always did a sound check wherever I was going to perform. I still do. This experience taught me never to make that mistake again. So I was standing in the wings and the stage manager said, "You're on." I said, "But I can't hear my music!" I couldn't hear it because it was outdoors. I was inside, the band was outside. I stood in the wings, petrified, afraid to go on. I could not hear the music during the whole show. It was horrible. It was a nightmare. Nobody applauded much. Offstage, I said, "Phyllis, get ready. The sound system has got to be fixed or changed." She said, "Don't worry about it." But she didn't get laughs.

After that show, I went to the orchestra leader and said, "I can't hear you. We've got to put speakers behind me. Anything. Something. I couldn't hear my music and it was scary as hell. It was like being deaf."

Even though we couldn't hear the orchestra and most of the audience couldn't hear us, I got good reviews! Later, it was wonderful singing with that orchestra, but that was one of the weirdest nights of my career. Now they have tremendous sound systems for outdoor performances, but then they weren't sophisticated enough to know how to do it. The idea was good and it looked beautiful out there but it was hell for the performer. The audience was getting it but the performers never knew what they were getting.

We were at the Shoreham for two weeks. We could never sleep because the guests communicated by banging on doors and they stayed up all night. What a gig!

I remember another night when Phyllis and I were performing at the Crescendo, a big club in Hollywood. She was at the peak of her popularity. Everybody came out, every big star in Hollywood. After each show, she invited me to her dressing room and we talked to everybody. I met everybody. This one night we were the last to

142

leave the club because so many people came back to see her, and we couldn't get out. Everything was locked. We could not get out of the place. It was scary. She said, "What if there's a fire? What will we do?" Neither of us was thinking positively at the moment. I thought I'd have to break a window. After we were in there for about an hour, getting more and more frantic, looking everywhere, the basement, the main floor, the kitchen, everywhere, finally, by some fluke, one of the workers came in and got us out.

Another night we were driving from a club to a hotel and Phyllis said, "Let's go have a hot dog." We drove up to a hot dog stand in the limo and had hot dogs and french fries. It was a riot.

Things only started to go wrong for Phyllis when she married the man who, I guess, is no longer her husband, Ward Donovan. She made a remark when she started to go out with Ward, who replaced me and whom she finally did marry. She said, "It could have been you." I was stunned. I didn't know that she was attracted to me. I thought we were great friends. I was always naïve about things like that. I never thought in those terms with whoever it was, male or female. Later, there were places where they wanted me back, or they didn't want Ward. She would call me and I'd go back on the road with her. It made him furious. But the business of show business is pleasing the management and the audience. If they don't want you back with another performer, you can't bring that one back. That's it.

In 1996, we were doing a benefit auction for the Singers Forum so I called Phyllis to ask for a donation. She asked, "How old are you now?" I said, "I'm seventy-two." And she said, "Oh, my God! Well, you'll always be thirty-eight to me." It was beautiful, the way she put it, that there is no age. Time stood still for us in 1962. I said, "Well, you'll always be thirty-five to me." Phyllis said, "You know, I get five requests a day for auctions. It's got to a place where I can't handle it, so we just throw them away." Then she said, "As soon as I hang up with you, I'm going to do it immediately so that it gets done." And, by God, she did. She sent a dress worth five thousand dollars. It was pink and embroidered with lovely beads all over. It was beautiful, very simple. In the box was a little book. I have it still. It's at the farm. It was a little souvenir book of her life that she sold. There was a note inside and there were autographed pictures and the note said, "My many faces." Her famous face lifts. She's still funny, positive. We had a great talk.

She's one of my great ladies for sure.

Eileen Farrell

Eileen Farrell is one of the great singers of all time. The thing about her that's very unusual is that she can sing opera and popular music equally well. Her opera is operatic, her pop is pop. I met her a long time ago, through friends, and we just hit it off. She has a wonderful family. One year, on Staten Island, they gave me an Italian birthday dinner. It was such a great evening. They were just like my family.

At some point, Eileen went to Indiana to teach voice. What a teacher she must have been! I caught up with her again when she came back to New Jersey, just over the Bridge. Physically, she's not very well. It's a balance problem. She says she feels like she's going to fall. In spite of that, she did another recording in London. She called it "My Last CD." She says there will not be any more. I don't know how she manages, feeling the way she does.

When we spoke about all this, I said to her, "Eileen, I had a wonderful idea. I want you to come to the Singers Forum, see the school and give a master class. Why don't you come with the CD and you'll give a talk and we'll ask questions. It would be so important for the students to get to hear you and know you." She said, "Oh, I would love that."

We started a series at the Forum called "Legends." Eileen is one of the legends.

Once Eileen was singing in Alice Tully Hall (or maybe Philharmonic Hall) and I went to hear her. I have never heard anybody sing like that, before or since. It was as if all the sound came out of her whole body. Her face was totally relaxed and I never felt the voice was coming out of her mouth. It was like natural stereophonic sound. I said, "Now that's what it's all about. That's a great singer!" She made such an impression on me. It showed me where the voice should come from. It's never your throat. It was just amazing. I'll never forget that. It was a revelation of a basic truth. I have loved her ever since.

She told me, when we last spoke, "I don't think you're going to recognize me. My hair is all white."

"Mine is too," I said.

Eileen's had a rough time. Besides her balance problem, her daughter was ill and then her son. But she's still singing. I think I'm her age, and I'm still singing, too.

Life for me seems to be coming full circle in so many, many ways. The people you really connect with, you don't lose. You can pick up with them right where you left off the last time. There's got to be a lot more to a relationship when that happens. It shows you that in life these things aren't just accidents. There is some reason why some people stay with you in your consciousness, not just because they're famous and wonderful performers. There has to be something that makes them stay with you, an energy, whatever you call it.

Everything about life is connections. The trick is, stay connected to the positive energies out there. Those are the energies that will always stay with you and take you wherever you want to go in this life. I have the feeling that I have known some people in another lifetime. It's the only way I can really understand it. There has to be something that was there before, or it wouldn't be that strong; people wouldn't be that willing to pick up with you where you left off. That's the feeling Eileen Farrell and I have between us. That continuity has to be there, somewhere, somehow.

Greta Garbo

I was walking through Central Park one day with Johnny King. It was a total surprise to me to see Greta Garbo strolling toward us. I said, "Oh, my God. That's Greta Garbo!"

Johnny said he had seen her many times, that she walked all over Manhattan, that she was always simply dressed, wore no makeup and paid no attention to gaping on-lookers, people who clutched their hearts and fainted at the sight of her, or screeching tires of suddenly halted taxis. And no one who had any class ever spoke to her.

I marched up to the lady and said, in my best baritone, "Oh, Miss Garbo, you're absolutely wonderful! Do you feel like talking?"

And, my hand to God, so help me, she said, "No, I want to be alone."

So I went on walking.

Johnny King has never forgiven me.

Ava Gardner

Was there a man in America who would have refused a request to take a gift to Ava Gardner from New York to London? If so, I wasn't one of them.

I was booked on a Sardi's tour to London, to spend Christmas in England, see some theater, dine at great restaurants, and stay at the Savoy, the most fantastic hotel in Europe. Don't ask me what year it was. I don't remember.

A friend who knew about the trip, asked me to take a Christmas gift from him to Ava Gardner, who was living in London at the time. Of course I said, "Yes!" After a day or two, I called on her and she was expecting me. The experience of being alone for an hour or so with the most beautiful woman in the world was disorienting, at the very least. And that voice!

The Christmas gift turned out to be cartons of her favorite cigarettes. This was probably illegal but in those days the British didn't X-ray you and your belongings on arrival at Heathrow. Ava ordered tea for two (!) and began to talk of New York Christmases. She had been ill and was lonesome. Then I brought her up to date on the latest backstage gossip. It was like having a chat over the back fence with a goddess.

I hated to leave but didn't want to wear her out, so I said my goodbyes and blew her a kiss, sadly, because I knew I had no excuse to come and see her again.

Nancy Kelly

It must be at least thirty years ago that I met the superb actress, Nancy Kelly. Charles Nelson Reilly introduced us. She'd had a long career in Hollywood and described herself to me as "Queen of the B Movies." She'd come to New York to get away from that and had tremendous successes in lead roles in *The Bad Seed* and *Who's Afraid of Virginia Woolf?* on Broadway.

Nancy then went back to Hollywood to repeat the mother's role in the movie of *Seed*. It was a hugely successful movie. She said she had really hoped to reenact her original role in *Who's Afraid*... but when Richard Burton got the role of the husband, Elizabeth Taylor got the part of the wife. Nancy was very disappointed and came back to New York.

Already established as a fine actress on stage and screen, Nancy studied with Lee Strasberg. We had kept up the acquaintance. She moved into a beautiful apartment at the St. Moritz. There was a Viennese restaurant on the ground floor, Rumpelmeyer's, where divorced fathers used to take their kids for ice cream after Sundays in the Park or at the Zoo.

When you visited Nancy, she led you directly to the kitchen, opened the fridge and said, "What can I feed you?" (That's just what my mother used to do at home in Buffalo; guests had to be fed on arrival.) I felt I was part of Nancy's family and she was part of mine. I tell you, it was a struggle to take her out to dinner. Sometimes we'd take my car to the East Side, to a great Chinese restaurant where "everybody" could be seen, a kind of early Asian "Elaine's." There were even places to park. It was a long time ago.

Nancy had married, then divorced, a very important

producer, Warren Caro, and had a daughter named Kelly. Nancy's mother had been, as she told me, a stage mother. Nancy'd had a lot of therapy to help her deal with that trauma. Kelly was a wonderful child of the Sixties. Nancy wasn't on her wave length at all. One time, Kelly went to our farm in Brocton and poured out her heart to my sister, Carolyn, and her husband, Mickey. I didn't pry but I thought it helped her. Carolyn and Mickey had such loving upbringings, and they just gave that love to Kelly.

Once Nancy gave me a birthday party. It must have been my forty-fifth. All our friends were there and we had such a great time. She ordered a cake from Rumpelmeyer's and it must have had lots of rum in it. That's all I remember of that party!

At the time, I was moving from performing to teaching full time. Nancy was very helpful. She used her long experience on stage and in movies to guide me. She shared her knowledge cheerfully, never condescendingly.

Nancy did TV in New York but the stage roles just weren't there. It made her unhappy. She became disillusioned about the profession. Having been at the top on Broadway and in Hollywood, she felt ignored and devalued. Finally she moved back to California and became very reclusive.

Nancy died in 1993. I had a little memorial service for her at home. I lit a candle for her and watched *The Bad Seed* and thought of all the wonderful times we'd had together. I called Kelly and we had a long talk about her mother. Kelly was married and the mother of two little girls.

I think the lack of roles for actresses over forty had a great deal to do with Nancy's unhappiness and disappointment. Things have changed a lot since those days. Katherine Hepburn, Lauren Bacall, Judi Dench and a dozen others are all working, winning awards, performing leading roles and having a hell of a good time. Movies, theater and TV are growing up, thank God. I only wish it had happened sooner.

A lot sooner.

Jacqueline Kennedy Onassis

When I moved to 87th Street & Central Park West, to the duplex apartment of my visualizations, I had the whole Park to play in. I started running every day, feeling better all the time. I had never smoked, seldom drank anything but a little wine, and watched my weight. Running was like returning to my childhood. It was always my sport.

Something else was contributing to getting me out the door every morning. Jackie Kennedy Onassis would run past me and we would smile and say, "Hi!" and I would be on Cloud Nine for the rest of the day. She had the most beautiful smile and she could say, "Hi!" better than anybody.

The only other place I ever saw her was at the Metropolitan Museum of Art, when I attended a special, black tie showing of the works of Monet. I somehow found myself in a small group of people being lectured to by the Museum's Director. There, standing next to him, was Ms. Onassis, magnificently dressed. She smiled at everybody, clearly enjoying the moment.

These days I walk briskly around Chelsea. It's healthy, but it's not the same.

Great Men

Charles Aznavour

In 1995, I went to Charles Aznavour's opening night on Broadway. It was a two-week engagement. I had met him when he performed at Carnegie Hall with Liza Minnelli. He is one of the most truly fascinating performers on the stage today, and has been for many years.

When he first became a performer, critics called him things like "puny," "unattractive," "grainy-voiced" and worse. They said he should stick to writing songs. They really put him down. Aznavour would not accept their put-downs. Now he is highly regarded, sought after as an actor, singer and writer of wonderful songs. He sings about love and life and all the things that everybody else sings about, but when he sings, the feelings are so deep you are absolutely enthralled. His grainy voice is coming out of his slender body, his less than handsome face, and the more you listen and watch, the more fascinating he becomes. You believe he has had these love affairs, had these broken hearts.

This opening night, I knew he was not well. He wasn't himself. I wondered what was wrong. The audience didn't seem to notice and he got his usual ovations. I wondered if he had come in late or tired from a long trip, or if he had a bad rehearsal. His voice was not right, nor his body language. Aznavour and I are the same age. I thought, *uh oh, is this how it happens when you're sev-*

enty-one? Is this how it ends?

I spoke to his manager and reminded him of our meeting, and said I'd love to see Charles. His manager said he was very ill, he's going right to his hotel, he's not going to see anyone tonight. He had a terrible bronchitis and he'd come in from Los Angeles and gotten very sick. I said, "God, the performance he gave! He didn't cut down on his energy or anything, but I knew." The manager asked me to come backstage another night. Then I got bronchitis, so I missed seeing him.

It's interesting how everything you are projects. That's why you really have to work on yourself, because everything about you is being picked up out there by someone. You'd better work on that positive energy because that's the only thing there is. Nothing else should exist when you're on stage. Negative energy must be dismissed because we can't be negative and give a good performance. The more I teach, the more I really see how everything in a person shows.

I once had a student, a tenor with a magnificent voice and a bad attitude. He could whoop out high As, Bs and Cs, I mean *full*. After a while I said to him, "You know, I hear what you're singing, but no one else will care that you are the great undiscovered tenor of this century. You have to get rid of that chip on your shoulder! The way you show your talent is through your voice, and how it affects your performance. You can't do that with a chip on your shoulder. No one wants to deal with belligerence. It's in your way."

Fortunately, he listened. He turned out to be such a warm person. The vulnerability he was hiding has come through. I'm glad that I could recognize it and help him with it, because that man, with one of the great voices, might have gone through his life that way and probably never have sung. Opera is hungry for men who can sing like him. He doesn't get tired up there. He just keeps going at those notes and now it's—wow!

Nat "King" Cole

Nat "King" Cole was the most disciplined and focused performer I have ever seen. I watched him every night for weeks at the Copacabana. Each number had its own moves, its own nuances, its own vocal inflections. Yet each number always appeared so easy, so fresh, so spontaneous. At every show, I felt that he was singing each song for the first time.

I learned a lot from the "King," especially that discipline is as important as voice for a career. His concentration made his presence and energy so compelling that you were drawn to him as if by a beam of light. Very few artists have had this power. I'm told that when Galli-Curci sang, you could hardly see her, the energy of light emanating from her was so intense. In my lifetime, I've personally seen this only rarely, in Garland, Dietrich, Helen Hayes, Geraldine Fitzgerald, Frank Sinatra, Joanne Woodward, and, of course, the "King."

Charles Nelson Reilly

Charles Nelson Reilly was starring in *How To Succeed in Business (Without Really Trying)* and teaching a musical theatre class at HB Studios in New York when I met him.

I had finished an engagement at the Fontainbleau Hotel in Miami and decided I wanted to go back to New York and study, reaffirm myself, find out who I was, where I was going, and start learning and growing all over again. I hadn't had a chance to take classes or anything for years because I was always out on the road. A friend of mine was raving about this musical theatre class at HB Studios where Charlie was teaching, so I thought, well, I'm going to check him out, go see the show. I did and I thought he was an absolutely brilliant actor. I knew I could learn things from this man. I joined the class and when he heard me sing, he practically fainted. I think he fell in love with my voice, and he took over like it was his voice. He was thrown by it. I guess a *bel canto* singer doesn't just wander into a musical theatre class very often.

I was a good actor. I was stage-wise. I was really good at it. The things that he gave me to do! I responded to the work and I still have notebooks that I made in his classes. The things he said were so meaningful to me that I just copied them down. I don't know if anyone else there did that, but I did and I refer to them often, because I learned more about acting from him than I ever learned from anybody except Lee Strasberg. Julie Harris says the same.

One day, Charlie said to me, "If and when you're ready for me to help you, just let me know." I was thrown. I wasn't used to that kind of thing. I usually did the helping.

So I thought about it and then one day I was near his apartment, going on my rounds. He had a phone but he never answered it. He had a thing about the phone. It was all part of his mystique. Charlie had a way of getting whatever he was after. He called it "duplicating," using the imaging process. He wanted the phone to ring with offers, but he wouldn't answer it. People would have to pursue him, to catch him at class or backstage. And it worked! He did *How To Succeed, Bye, Bye, Birdie, Hello,*

Dolly! and *Skyscraper* on Broadway, all in a row. He believed people wanted him more because he wasn't waiting for the phone to ring. He was right.

So I appeared at his apartment and said, "I'm ready. Let's do it."

He started to get me work and he started to talk to everybody about me and that really was the big plus of my career. It was tremendous. It was the most rewarding, exciting time for me, because it really brought me into the theater and the theater crowd: everything I wanted. It was just great. I decided to stay in New York. I wanted theater and musical comedy and when all this hype Charlie was putting out got around town, I was hired for the road company of *I Can Get It For You Wholesale,* the show that made Barbra Streisand famous. It was a great part. I was out on the road again but the show wasn't a big hit out of town. It was a very "New York" show.

Then I came back to class and a summer of singing and studying. Don Morrow, one of Charlie's friends, was an emcee on a big quiz show on TV, a very nice man. He had a club called Wheel and Compass in West Hampton, on Long Island. It was right on the water and it was a wonderful club. Charlie brought me to Don and said, "You've got to have Andy sing at your club on weekends." Don was all for it. Charlie was a great agent. I stayed with Don and his wife in their beach house on weekends. It was the most fabulous summer. People heard about my singing and came from everywhere. I used the whole club. I did very theatrical things. I used different hats that I hung on an old hat stand for different songs. I would finish the act singing "Ebb Tide" as I walked out through the doors right to the ocean. It was the talk of the town. These were all new things that I did that were stimulated by my work with Charlie. There was a woman who came in

155

every Friday and Saturday night. She worked in TV and she had a beautiful little white poodle. I sang a song, "Nobody's Heart Belongs To Me," and I'd pick up the dog and sit on a stool and sing to it. I had the best time. Everybody cried! Again!

Everyone came there. Charlie came on Saturday nights after his show, with Robert Morse, then the star of *How To Succeed*. ... Then Bobby got in my corner. He and I would do "You're The Top" as a duet. He was (and is) such a star. He was very hyper, very funny, and I never realized that he was drinking until he talked about it himself. Sunday nights, before we all went back to New York, I'd get them up to do stuff. It was fun. The place was always jammed because everyone knew somebody big would be there. It was the place to be. We'd all stay with the Morrows. Sometimes we'd go back with Don late on Sunday, and they'd all go back to work on Monday. I was there all summer and great people like Linda Lavin would come out. I'd bring out people from the classes that I had worked up scenes with, and Johnny King and I had developed a number sitting at a bar, drinking and we would do it right at the bar in the club. I think the song I used was "Here's That Rainy Day." Nell Webster came, too, a girl who was like Carol Burnett, classy and funny. We had worked up some numbers, too. People never knew what they were going to get. All these people were good. It was a wonderful summer, so we did it the following summer, too. Then Don gave up the club and moved to Mexico. He was very smart about investing so maybe he'd made enough money by then. David Hedison, the actor, came out. He was an old friend of Charlie's. Peter Marshall, too, the man who did "Hollywood Squares," and Alan Ludden, another actor and quiz show host, who married Betty White.

It was around this time that Bobby Morse and Charlie got me on a TV show with Jim Backus. He had a format that introduced new talent, new faces, on TV. Somebody famous had to bring you on. So Charlie and Bobby brought me on and there was a set of part of an airplane, with me in a trench coat, carrying an attaché case up the steps to the plane's door. I sang "I Left My Heart In San Francisco," the first time it was heard on TV. I think I still have a copy of the tape somewhere.

While all this was going on, Charlie had worked up an act for me called "The Party's Over" to use when I performed at the Bon Soir, a club in Greenwich Village. It was rather melancholy but people loved to cry and so I went on with it. Charlie did another great thing for me the night I opened at Bon Soir. He borrowed the Sardi family's red British double-decker bus, put all his famous friends on it after their shows closed, and drove them to the club. How I got through that opening night I'll never know. It was pandemonium from start to finish.

I got the Bon Soir job as a result of the efforts of a group of Italian men who had seen me in the Fountainebleau GiGi Room, and liked my work. I played there often and really enjoyed it. My "management team" was wonderful to me. I made money for them. We had a great time. They loved my singing. They were proud of me and gave me wonderful engagements. This was part of the excitement for Charlie, too, I think. I used to wonder what he got from me. Maybe I was the only Sicilian person he knew! This period was so exciting and brought a lot of sparkle to his life (and mine). He was really carried away. These were absolutely wonderful people who were very kind and loving and really helped me tremendously. I thought of them as my "uncles." It was almost like being a teenager again. It was an opening up, such an opening up of my entire being. I was stretching as a performer, as a singer, as an actor, and it was exactly what I wanted when I left Florida, knowing that I had to go back to New York City and find myself. All of that was happening at the same time, and it was a happy time.

While I was taking from Charlie, I would go to auditions to get jobs of all kinds, in and out of town, to pay for classes. One time I even took a job as a messenger, and met some wonderful people living in gorgeous places while doing it. Any way at all, I wanted to take Charlie's classes, dance classes, classes in everything there was to know about show business.

Aspiring artistes, beware! College, Conservatory, bachelor's and master's degrees are only the beginning. Visualize yourselves as life-long students. It's the only way to keep your skills sharp and up-to-date. I really learned this and I feel strongly about it. I study still. My students hear it from me early and often.

One day, after class, I said to Charlie, "I love working with you. I hate having to go out of town to earn the money to come back and take from you. It's driving me nuts."

Charlie, who never missed much, had seen my degrees from the New England Conservatory of Music. He said, "Why don't you teach?"

I was floored. Why hadn't I thought of that? Such a simple sentence, a simple idea. It changed my life and, I firmly believe, saved it.

My reply was, "I'm going to have to buy a piano!" The prospect terrified me. Charlie had that look in his eye that he got whenever he found himself dealing with other people's neuroses.

Charlie and I went immediately to a piano store to look at second-hand instruments. Actually, I had seen a picture of a piano and fallen in love with it. I had even visualized it being in my West 73rd Street apartment, in front of the big bay window in the living room. And there it was!

Panic took over. Years of penny-pinching gripped my brain. I relived the entire Depression in a flash. Inside, I was screaming, "How am I going to pay for it and help my family and eat and pay rent and go to Charlie's classes?" I mumbled, "I can't afford it."

Charlie didn't lose his temper, though it cost him. He said, "I'll send you students. Everything will be fine." So I silenced my fear, bought the piano on the never-never, and it came to my living room to sit in front of the bay window. I sat down next to my phone with a pen and my appointment book and visualized pages full of students' names, phone numbers and appointments.

For weeks, Charlie checked in on the hour to see how I was doing. He recommended me to A.M.D.A., a fine school then in the Ansonia Hotel, to substitute for Lehman Engel, the famous Broadway conductor. Then the Clark Center for the Arts needed someone. Charlie heard about it. I had an interview and got the job. My classes there became huge. Charlie helped to put together ads for the paper, "Show-Business." They were really good.

Then Geraldine Fitzgerald became my private student and when I thought she was ready to perform in front of a class, I staged the title song from *Coco* for her. Three men representing her lovers did most of the singing. Geraldine stepped out in her tam o'shanter, a fisherman's wool sweater and a plaid skirt, radiant as always, and repeatedly spoke the word "Coco" on beat and on pitch, and the electricity in her voice as she lived the emotions of the character sent chills through us all.

She got an ovation and Geraldine discovered she had a whole new career before her. My world exploded into new galaxies, new possibilities.

Then Charlie started to have a hard time deciding whether to move to California for the TV series, *The Ghost and Mrs. Muir*, when it was offered to him. I think by that time he was probably getting tired of spending so much energy on me, too. He had to do something new with his career. He was so nervous about that decision that his apartment was permeated with the conflict he felt. He couldn't decide. His cat and I were like his emotional punching bags. That cat had a habit of walking on the wide wall that ran around the penthouse apartment. I would see this and take the cat down and put it inside. This one day the cat jumped up on the wall and over the side, down twenty stories, and I fainted. I just fell over. I couldn't move. I thought I was dying. Charlie was heartbroken about the cat and worried about me.

Charlie moved to California and did the show and was successful in everything he did there, commercials and doing Johnny Carson's show and a lot of stuff, but he really wanted to direct, and now he's doing it extremely well, like he does everything. He's still teaching, too. His students are so lucky.

Hollywood is a dangerous place. People go there thinking that the picture or show they've got will make them for life, but it doesn't often happen that way. It is, to put it mildly, a crap shoot. I visited Charlie and we went up to San Francisco. I met Dick Van Dyke then, and his great family. Charlie had put me together with Phyllis Diller before he left New York, and I was touring with her, too.

I can't thank Charles Nelson Reilly enough for his generosity and support during what could have been a miserable time in my life. I consider him a good friend even though our paths haven't crossed much recently.

In 1997, when he directed Julie Harris and Charles Durning in *Gin Game* and won a Tony, Charlie was backstage when I went to say hello to Julie. He was still the same, except older, and very lively. He was very warm, very affectionate. I asked him to do a master class for the Singers Forum. He's such a brilliant director. What he did with *Gin Game* was great. Julie loves working with him. She says he's the best director she's ever had and the best teacher, too. I fully agree with her. He is a wonderful teacher. He taught me so much about acting and the theater. No one ever taught me the things he did about musical comedy.

I took classes from other teachers and I really concentrated on acting later on, for about two years, while I was working in clubs. Teaching allowed me to do that. Charlie sent me lots of his students. I took from Walt Whitcover for a time and I studied with Herbert Berghof's protégé, Michael Beckett, who is now teaching at the Singers Forum. Then, when I met Geraldine Fitzgerald, she encouraged me to stay with Michael. We bartered my singing lessons for his staging me at Alice Tully Hall. All this was going on while I studied with Charlie.

The last time I saw him, backstage, he looked fine. It was like going back to another lifetime. I had such a strong connection to Charlie, but there's a feeling now that we have parted ways. It makes me sad.

Frank Sinatra and Sammy Davis, Jr.

If you've ever had the experience of having to do something seemingly impossible and surviving, you've learned that you can do anything. The years of the Depression, of having to face landlords and bill collectors and tell them what they didn't want to hear so they wouldn't evict us or sue us, taught me I could take any bull by the horns and live through it.

When I was fifteen or sixteen, I heard Frank Sinatra was coming to Buffalo to sing at the Shea's Theater. I knew I wanted to meet him.

Sinatra had been on radio in Buffalo, through the Mutual Network. I remember hearing him for the first time when I was about fourteen and thinking, "I can do that!" I had just won a contest and the prize was a week at Shea's Theater, singing with Les Brown and his band. It was a wonderful prize and an unbelievable experience for a fourteen-year-old. But I knew all the popular songs and I'd had a great time.

When Sinatra came to town, I went through the alleyway to his backstage dressing room. I knocked on the door and he said, "Okay, come," and I did. He was alone. He was very thin and so was I. He was a Sicilian and so was I. I thought, *What could go wrong?* I asked him for his autograph and he gave it to me graciously. Then I told him I loved his voice, that I wanted to be a singer too but I was waiting for my voice to change. He said, "Kid, that's a great idea." He was so nice. He just took the time for me. I didn't stay long but when I left, I felt like I was flying.

Many years later, I was working at the Copacabana in New York City, as the production singer. It was a wonderful job. I worked two shows every night and three on Saturdays, for months, doing the same routines with the beautiful Copa girls. I had that job for a long time. Jules

Podell, the owner, reigned supreme there. I had auditioned for him and then I just hounded that man. I called him from the farm. I called him from everywhere. I just wanted that job! It was a wonderful opportunity because I worked with all the big names at the time: Nat King Cole, Sammy Davis, Jr., Jack Carter. There were so many that I don't remember them now, all the big headliners in the business. None of them were as easy to get to know as Sammy Davis, Jr. He was very generous. He would take you out after the show and feed you and he'd always have a big group of people. He was married to Mai Britt at the time and she didn't seem too happy about it all. I never did get to know her but I got to know Sammy. Later on, he was doing the play, *Desperate Hours,* on Long Island, in summer stock. It was just after opening night. There weren't that many people backstage when I came in. Sammy was very upset. I said, "What's wrong?"

He said, "When I came here to see Tallulah Bankhead do a play, she had an oriental rug on the floor of this dressing room. When I came to work, it was gone." He was upset because, understandably, he thought it was the race issue.

I said, "Sammy, if you want an oriental rug, you must put that in your contract. Tallulah Bankhead had that in her contract, I'm sure. It sounds like she wanted an oriental rug and she demanded it."

It sounded logical to him. Then I said, "Next time, put it in your contract." That made him feel better.

One evening, I came into work at the Copa and the place was buzzing like a disturbed wasps' nest. Usually, in the late afternoon, things were pretty quiet, so I asked a waiter, "Why all the uproar?"

He said, "Frank Sinatra's coming to the show tonight."

I said, "And?"

He said, "Mr. Sinatra tips hundred dollar bills."

When I stepped out on stage to sing to an audience that included Frank Sinatra, I was nervous, but I had gotten used to celebrities coming in. They were always there. That was one reason I wanted to sing at the Copa. I wanted to get into that milieu and I wanted to meet those people. It was exciting at every show.

That night, after the first show, I was invited to sit at the Sinatra table with his other guests. Again, he was so nice to me. It was just like sitting at anybody's table. He was very low key. He didn't come on as the great star he was. It was all very easy talk with a lot of people. It was a table for eight. I wish I could remember more but when that happens to you, it's such a moment in time, it's so powerful that you can't always grab it because it goes by so fast. You're just in some euphoric state. Not that I wasn't aware of what was going on, but it's hard to explain it. You want to make an impression and you don't want to make a fool of yourself. Then half-hour is called, and you have to go get made up and into costume and go back to work.

Frank Sinatra was a role model for many singers. Until he appeared on the scene, there were no Italian popular singers of any importance. The bands were the big deal. Singers came in a distant second, most often harmonizing in easily interchangeable groups. When Frank Sinatra broke the mold, he created a professional life for many singers. I'm sure I got the "Armed Forces Mail Call" show in 1942 because of his success. I was 4F in the draft, skinny, Sicilian, and sang sweetly. How could they lose? Aside from all those good things, I had drive, I loved to sing, I loved to work hard. I didn't have the street smarts that you needed to become a star, or the street fighter's instincts. I would not have wanted to live Sinatra's life. The more I see of celebrities, the more I see that's not really the way I would have wanted to go. You don't have any privacy. You're surrounded by bodyguards. Your personal life is fodder for trash magazines and you have no way of stopping it. Sinatra lived that way. There are stars who have figured out how to live normally, and there are stars who choose not to, who need the chaos and the adulation, who can't live without it. After Sinatra died, a cousin of his was quoted as saying that Sinatra was very lonely as a child. Sometimes, when this cousin stayed over, he'd hear him crying at night. That could have been the reason he needed people around him all the time. He couldn't be alone.

I have loved my life. I wouldn't have lived it any other way.

Lee Strasberg

In the late '60s, I was teaching speech to an aspiring actress. She was very Greek, very passionate, full of feelings. She just flipped over everything I taught. She told me, "My God, you have got to meet Lee! You're just like Lee! You talk like Lee!" In New York, in those days, if anyone in show business said, "Lee!" everyone else knew they meant Lee Strasberg.

I said I would love to meet Lee. She said, "You should be teaching for Lee!" I said, "Well, if you tell him about me, I'll be glad to meet him and talk to him."

Well, she did speak to Lee, probably using even more exclamation points, and I went downtown to the Institute. It was a small place, just a few little rooms on 13th Street. At that time he taught only acting at the Institute.

We met and I told him about my career, what I had done, what I was doing. He liked the fact that I was still performing and teaching simultaneously. He said, "That's very good. Very important." I told him about my background and what I taught in singing and speech, what my method was, how I did it.

Away from the classroom and his own living room, Lee Strasberg had the reputation of saying next to nothing. Well, he was anything but monosyllabic that day. He said, "When I was an actor, way back, I was sent out for a role in a play. I knew I had to work on my voice. I went to a teacher someone had recommended and the things you're telling me are the things he told me." The teacher had shown him an exercise. He put Lee up against a wall, aligning his spine and head, and stepped away. Then the teacher said, "Lift the chest as you're speaking and get louder, and as you lift the chest, tip the head slightly down."

I couldn't believe it. I said, "Well, that's it. That is the covering of the voice, the *bel canto*...That's how you get projection."

Lee was very excited. I had confirmed his faith in what he'd learned early in the 1920's, the basis of the *bel canto* technique.

Lee hired me on the spot, to start the voice/ singing/ speech department at the Institute. I said I'd have to bring in another teacher because I couldn't handle all that. Lee said, "I want you to do whatever you want to do. You set it up and do it your way and whatever you want to get paid, you'll get paid."

All I asked for was whatever I was getting at the time, an hourly rate, and transportation. I think it was more than any other teacher was paid. I never, ever, had another conversation with Lee about the mechanics of my classes. He left me in total charge. Everything started to happen and he was thrilled.

I brought John Harris in to do the speech classes. I did voice/singing classes. We had such enormous numbers of students, I couldn't have given them all private lessons. I formulated the voice curriculum. John Harris formulated the speech classes.

One day, John was having trouble with a restless speech class. He said, in his most *bel canto* authoritative tones, "Everybody! Lie down on the floor!" They were so shocked they actually did it. Then he said, "Close your eyes. Breathe through your mouth." Later John told me he was inspired by God.

From there on, John and I built the meditation system, the breathing pattern. I was excited by the control of the classes it gave us. We developed the very special warmup we use to this day, to start classes, get students to concentrate, breathe effectively and think of their artistic goals, before every class. Our students do it before performances, before auditions, just to start the day.

Lee Strasberg gave me unlimited support. I went often to his home and got to know his wife, Anna, and the children, friends, students and co-workers. There, Lee did the talking. He was fascinating. He had so much to say, all of it interesting.

There has been endless talk about "the Method" and the Actors Studio, the mumbling and the scratching. In Lee's classes, there was nothing like that. When he did scenes from musical theatre, he did them exactly as I would have done them. At the Actors Studio, you had to audition to get in, but you didn't have to study with Lee. Marlon Brando, James Dean and others made people think he taught the "torn tee shirt" style of acting, but he never did.

What Lee taught was that the internal life of the actor should be used to light the stage. There, an actor must perform a script night after night, month after month, sometimes for years. Unless you have an internal and personal framework to perform from, you become mechanical, flat and tired. Lee didn't play true confessions. He wanted his students to look inside themselves for an emotion they experienced in real life and use the feelings it made you remember to get the real substance of the part out there on stage in a scene, a play, a song. I learned so much about acting from Lee.

Students paid a thousand dollars for a ten or twelve week session with Lee, an enormous amount of money at the time. It was THE thing in New York. Everyone who did get in his classes felt very important.

I have such wonderful feelings, thinking and writing about Lee Strasberg. I love being in the presence of knowledge. I've always been a very good student. I believe in being a student for my entire lifetime. I always find it strange when people tell me they're beyond being a student. I don't know what they mean. I have been learning all my life.

I met Lee when he was in his late sixties. In the 1970s, Al Pacino got Lee a part in *Godfather II* and Lee absorbed the techniques and mechanics of acting on a sound stage in front of a camera. At the same time, he was teaching acting classes on both coasts. He died in 1982, when he was eighty-one, after a lifetime in the theater, as actor, teacher and movie star.

Now THAT'S impressive!

Metaphysics

When I started to take piano lessons from my Aunt Lena, I treated her like she was a big deal and she liked it. She was my first music teacher. She and her husband, Uncle Charlie, my step-grandmother, Caterina's, son, did start to come around more to our house and to my grandfather's farm. The family didn't quite understand Aunt Lena. No one really did, including my parents. I always stood up for her. Nobody else did, except for her mother-in-law.

We got very close, my aunt and uncle and me. Aunt Lena was attractive and fascinating. She kept you mesmerized with any story she told. She had a crippled leg and limped, but she was so lively and interesting, I never noticed it. I didn't see her that much after I started to take singing lessons. I was torn between staying friendly with her after Caterina died, or with the rest of the family. They didn't like her and I didn't know how to hold on to my feelings for her.

Recently, I found a book Aunt Lena gave me when I was about fourteen. It's called, *Every Man A King, Might in Mind Mastery,* by Orrison Swett Marden. It started me in metaphysics. I looked inside, and it says, "With the Assistance of Ernest Raymond Holmes." Ernest Holmes is the man who began "Science of Mind Thought." He was the founder of the church that my later metaphysics teacher, Raymond Charles Barker, was a minister at.

This book was first given to C. Samuel Barone. On the fly leaf is written, "To C. Samuel Barone. 'The fault, dear Brutus, lies not in our stars but in ourselves.' March, 1939, Sincerely, E. Rotunda." Rotunda was a well-known name out in Brocton. Then Aunt Lena has written: "There are three kinds of people in this world, the wills, the won'ts and the can'ts. The first, the wills, accomplish everything. The second, the won'ts, oppose everything, and the can'ts fail at everything."

This book was published first in 1906, and my copy is the 1935 edition. The publishers were Thomas Y. Crowell and mine is the fortieth printing. It's very precious to me. Mr. Rotunda gave it to Sam Barone, who gave it to Aunt Lena, who gave it to me, and it started me on my path to metaphysics.

Sam Barone was a very handsome man who grew up in Dunkirk, near the farm. He had a very strong mother and it was hard for him to escape from her. He had two sisters. When I was growing up, he always created such excitement among the females whenever he came around. I mean, ye gods! I know Aunt Lena was attracted to him. He did leave Dunkirk for Boston and graduated from an important Boston drama school. Sam helped me because he talked about Boston and college and all of that, and it got me interested and excited about what I'd do when I finished high school.

The next step on the path to metaphysics was an illness. I was sick for two weeks, alone in New York. The only book I had in the apartment that I hadn't read was a text book *Science of Mind,* by Ernest Holmes. It was given to me by Leon Leonardi, the conductor for Mimi Benzell, the Metropolitan Opera star, when we were all working in Chicago. Leon and I had some discussions about Ernest Holmes and he knew the book would help me, but as a Catholic, I wasn't ready for it then. This time I was. It's fabulous. Everything is in that textbook. When I read it, I said, "Oh, God, this is it!"

Then I started to go to the Science of Mind Church and met Raymond Charles Barker, the minister, and began to take his classes. This was during the real "spiritual hippy" movement. I finally did a daily concert program at St. Peter's Church in Manhattan and all around New Jersey. It was a program of spiritual songs, first giving a talk about the songs and what the songs meant to me, then singing the songs. The Broadway shows *Godspell* and *Jesus Christ, Superstar* were very hot then.

This particular Sunday in New Jersey, my regular pianist couldn't come, so the church brought in a lady who played the organ there. When I arrived, I went into the minister's room, hung up my coat and went to rehearse. At the organ sat someone who looked familiar. I said, "Aunt Lena?" When she saw me, she said, "S-S-Sandy?" and fainted. Oh, my God, it was such a dramatic moment. I had two carloads of people with me from New York and they all helped take care of her. It was moving and wonderful.

Aunt Lena had had no idea it was me she'd be playing for. Talk about full circle! So we went over the songs, but instead of giving my usual talk, I spoke to the congregation about Aunt Lena. I told them about her and about life and its rewards, that love never dies, how my love for her was strong, how wonderful it was that this had happened in their church. After the concert was over, I said, "I must see my uncle." Aunt Lena called and told Uncle Charlie I was there, what had happened and that I wanted to see him. Then I got on and said, "There's so many people with me. I'll pick up some food and we'll come to your house." Uncle Charlie said, "Oh, that would be lovely."

Uncle Charlie was standing in the driveway when I,

and my two carloads of people, got there. He was smiling, and so warm. He was still handsome. I got out of the car and the scene was right out of an Italian movie. We were so full of feelings, nobody knew what to do. They just stood there, motionless, watching us. He had his arm on my shoulder for this whole beautiful day. Their house made such an impression on me. It had tall windows, looking out to trees and woods. It was very modern and had a big skylight that lit up a little greenhouse filled with flowers and trees in planters. They still had their two Steinway grand pianos in the living room. There were Italian ceramic tables and pedestals with flowers on them. I had never seen anything so beautiful in my life. She told me they were from Genori's in New York, and even though I couldn't afford it, I went and bought a table as soon as I got back to the city. It stands in my present home there and tells me of a time when miracles did happen.

When I told my mother what had happened, she was thrilled. She said she wanted to see Charlie, who was her step-brother, but she never let me call them when she was in New York so they could get together. I was afraid to do it on my own because my mother could have had a heart attack. Every time she came to see me, I would say. "Do you want me to call Uncle Charlie?"

She would say, "No."

I knew she wanted to see him, desperately. They loved each other. But she wouldn't, I think because my Aunt Lena had taken him away, and that, to her, was that.

Long before I knew there was such a thing as metaphysics, I always felt more at home on the stage than off. I was always comfortable there, even as a little boy. I didn't have any trouble talking on stage, feeling my songs, expressing myself in the songs. Granted, some of them were imagined feelings then, but when I got older, I wanted to express real feelings. I wanted to find the ways of doing that. It's what I'm teaching now. That's why I came back to New York, went back to school when I was in my forties. Then I was still doing the "Vegas" act. You get out there and you knock 'em dead. You give out. I wasn't really expressing myself from inside. Some things were coming through because I was relaxed on stage and I was enjoying it and finding it easy to do. But I knew that I had to go deeper. I first made the connection between performing and using adult feelings when I met Tony Bennett. Even though I had already been exploring metaphysics, there was something new about the book, *The Art Of Loving,* that his coach, Michael Brown, told me to read. I saw how Tony had opened up. I think he had gone into analysis around that time and I knew that's what I had to do because I knew I wasn't really putting it all out there. I think that when I did my work at St. Peter's, I really did put it out there and that's what that was for. I had feelings that I put into my music at that time that were unbelievable. People came with boxes of Kleenex and cried and cried. My friend, Robert Morse, was one of those who came. He said, "I've never cried so much in the middle of the afternoon in my life." Every time I opened my mouth they cried. The feelings and the sound were so powerful. I was using the words of songs in an acting way to arrive at those feelings. A lot of it just came spontaneously. I went through a very painful period because I was opening up. My headaches got worse. At eleven o'clock in the morning, I'd get into a taxi to go to St. Peter's. Then I'd have the driver stop, I'd open the door, throw up into a storm drain and then we'd go on. I was opening up so much, my body couldn't take it. The material was spiritually and vocally so demanding. It was an amazing couple of years. I had no idea it would be so successful. I wasn't being paid. It was the first time in my life that I wasn't getting paid for singing. That allowed me the luxury of doing and saying and feeling, because I couldn't get fired. I wasn't doing it for me. I was doing it for St. Peter's Church. They got the money and paid my musicians. It was a big step. I got over the feeling I had, that I was a working singer so I must be paid! I did it for the love of doing it. It was a bit like when I used to sing as a child, but even then I got paid. They threw money at me! But now, because I wasn't paid money, I was paid in greater ways. I got fabulous reviews! I ended up on TV news with Pia Lindstrom. I had learned that there are rewards in giving it all away, that you have to keep everything circulating, that if what you want is to receive, you've got to give. If you want money, you've got to give money. If you want help, you've got to give help. You create a circulation between two opposites. They're the same thing, giving and getting. If you want to get love, you've got to give love.

I think that's where my maturity started. I have never backed away from that. I keep looking for ways in my teaching and in myself to keep opening up all those feelings and ways to express them on stage. You can't cry all the time. You can't fake joy. It has to be real joy. You have to get it across that feelings are what life is about.

I remember feeling lonely and misplaced as a kid, and after I read *Every Man A King* I felt there was no one I could talk to but my Aunt Lena.

It was always in my mind. It started me into visualization. I visualized myself going to college, going to that radio station, going to the Conservatory in Boston. All of that really came from, and was prompted by, *Every Man*

A King. I've always been, it seems, ahead of my time, in the way I felt about singing and show business and teaching, and all of the things that I've pursued in my career, moving from one kind of music to another, wanting to do it all. Show business puts people in categories. I felt I had no category, because I felt music is music and you should sing all of it!

Great Art

While I lived in the brownstone at 73rd & Riverside Drive, I visualized the place I really wanted to live in. For me, part of the process involves finding pictures that approximate what I want, so I can see them in my mind's eye.

I found my ideal apartment in a magazine. It belonged to a record producer, Bob Crewe, whom I later met and became friendly with. There was the piano I had dreamed of, and finally bought at Charlie Reilly's urging. There were fabulous paintings on the walls, works of modern artists mostly, Corot, Picasso and other Impressionists. I thought, "I could be happy in this room. I will be happy in this room!"

My dear Maureen McNally and her husband, Claude Giroux, had to leave for a long stay in Europe. It was a last minute situation and they had no way to safely store their collection of, guess what? You're right! Modern artists: Corot, Picasso, etc. They said, "Please take them and hang them and love them till we come back."

I never said "Yes!" faster.

They appeared with a cab full of paintings, helped me carry them upstairs and went off to Europe with no worries about their art. It was safe with me. No art thief worth a damn would think of such a treasure being in my little apartment in a somewhat shabby brownstone on the second floor. John Harris came by and we spent the day hanging all the paintings. They seemed almost to arrange themselves in the proper order. I realized I had an art gallery in my apartment and a fine grand piano, just as I had visualized them, using Bob Crewe's place as my image.

When Maureen and Claude reclaimed their cherished collection, I was about to move because I had seen the murderer of a young neighbor as he came down the stairs after killing her. I had to move. A top floor duplex, with a terrace on Central Park West, was handed on to me by a dear friend and student, Beverly Hayes, and I soon began my own cherished art collection. It doesn't equal or even come close to the Girouxes Impressionists, but I love it and it's mine.

More Great Art

In the early 1980's, I traveled to Italy to experience Italian opera in its native setting. One day I was in the Rome railroad station, waiting for a train to Milan. La Scala is the Mecca of the opera world. All true believers hope to go there at least once and I was a true believer.

The station was bustling, busy with the masses of summer tourists and year-round Italians crisscrossing Italy. A woman waiting on the same platform, wearing a smart white suit and hat, carrying a small makeup case, stood out. She was beautiful and seemed vulnerable, sad. I greeted her and said I was a voice teacher from New York, on a busman's holiday to La Scala. I wanted her voice to be low and sultry. It was. She said she had been vacationing at her summer place near Lugano and had been called back for a few days.

I sensed that underlying sadness and wondered what her life was like. She was obviously comfortably established. It seemed she wanted to talk to someone and I was there, a total stranger from another country, and willing to listen. We shared a compartment and began our conversation. We were at ease with one another. She had a rich, low voice and spoke excellent English, much better than my Italian. Her slight Italian accent gave our talk an aura of mystery and intrigue.

She told me her name but I'll keep that secret. She was in a failing marriage, with a teenage son away at school. She doted on him. Her father was head of an extremely important Italian business. Using his clout, he had helped the now-straying husband to a successful career. So far, it seemed like a not-unusual modern day story: upwardly mobile gent meets and marries the boss's daughter, finds room at the top and doesn't need her any more.

When we got to Milan, it seemed to both of us that we hadn't finished talking. I suggested we have dinner together. We did and she didn't want the evening to end. We exchanged phone numbers and went our separate ways.

Next day, she invited me to tea at her apartment. (Think Trump Tower, without the rococo garnish.) It was incredibly simple, the best Italian modern, splashes of color accenting steel and leather. A balcony overlooked the city. When the tea tray was removed, the lady said, "Because you are an artist of the voice and you appreciate all creative art, I am going to show you some paintings. Only a few people have seen them, people I can trust."

She walked to a wall, opened a concealed door and revealed a room that was really a bank vault. Stacked against the walls were paintings by great Italian masters of the ages. She brought them out, one at a time, for me to appreciate in the proper light. There were about twenty, maybe twenty-five, canvasses of different sizes. For me, time passed in slow motion. I was absolutely stunned. All I could feel was pity that she couldn't hang them on her walls. When I said so, she replied, sadly, "In Italy, you can't." I said the building and her apartment seemed to have quite up-to-date security. Again, she said, "In Italy—" and shrugged. I asked, "Why do you trust me, a man you've never seen before? I could be an imposter, a thief, a con man." She said, "No, you are none of those things. Trust me. I am well acquainted with a con man."

179

I can't describe how I felt. The beauty and grandeur of centuries-old paintings, hidden in darkness behind a bomb-proof door, overwhelmed me. I felt so sad for the artists who created them. Did they know their priceless works might never be shown, that the world has no place where they can hang safely?

That last day we talked mostly of her father and how much she loved him, and her young son. We kept in touch for a long time. I haven't heard from her recently. I can only hope that her collection is still in its protective steel womb, waiting to be reborn into a safer, sweeter world.

The "Uncles"

When I was still in my teens, the husband of a relative of my mother's saw the money value of what I could do, even then. He had great ideas but no money to do it himself. He wanted to exploit my talent. He told me of a girl about my age, who later became a great star and a good friend, but I won't tell you her name. He said "they" were starting her off in a not-too-distant city and she was really doing great. He wanted to present me to "them." I knew my parents would never agree to my leaving high school and going to another city. When he raised it with them, they shot the idea down in no uncertain terms. They didn't approve of this man at all, but they didn't tell me why.

Another time, a man had heard me sing, either through "Armed Forces Radio" or some other engagement. He, too, saw dollar signs. He wanted to take me to New York. I said, "You'll have to talk to my parents." He arrived at our house on a Sunday morning as we were going to church, so he came with us. He really was clever. He put a ten-dollar bill (then, it would feed a family of five with a dog and a cat for a week!) in the collection plate so we would all see it and be impressed. I was, but my parents weren't. He came to Sunday dinner and he was very charming. He made his pitch. My father would not hear of it. He never said why, but his native intelligence told him I would be used by people with their own agendas, and if I wasn't a miraculous money maker, they'd drop me. My father wanted me to study, to learn my craft and make a life for myself, and he and my mother were in complete agreement.

Questions like, "What would have happened if they said yes?" didn't occur to me till I started writing this book. Another question: "What did these two men really want of me, a raw eighteen-year-old, naïve, religious and family-oriented?" Another question, "Who were the 'they' these men referred to?"

When I was doing "Armed Forces Radio" and going to college, I got a professional gig at a Niagara Falls restaurant. It was only a bus ride from Buffalo. I worked there on Friday and Saturday nights. A very glamorous woman—Shirley was her name—played piano for me. There was no orchestra, just Shirley and me.

One of the customers came in every Friday and Saturday night and sat alone at a table. She looked like Hedy Lamar, wore Hollywood-style clothes and a turban. This was hot stuff in 1940. She ordered dinner and drinks for herself. She never smiled. I was so naïve. I asked the bartender why she came alone and why she never smiled. The man just shrugged, so I guessed he thought it was none of my business. She began inviting me to her table between sets and I discovered why she didn't smile: she had very bad teeth. It seemed odd to me that so lovely a woman wouldn't take care of her teeth. We would talk and then I'd do my set. God knows what she saw in me. One night she offered to drive me to my bus stop. I mentioned it to the bartender. He said, "Look, I better warn you. She is the girl friend of the big Mafia don here in Niagara Falls. You really should cool it because it could make a big problem for you."

Eighteen not being the brightest age, I did let her drive me that one time, but I realized I was in over my head and I didn't do it again.

That was my first encounter with a gorgeous woman with a murky past. I'll never understand why she picked on me. When she stopped coming to the restaurant. I was very relieved.

I was beginning to understand who "they" were.

Miami

I used to visit Gretchen Wyler, the musical comedy star of
Can Can and other big shows, and her husband in War-
wick, New York, (believe me, this is relevant) where they
had a house and a collection of classic cars. He had a
Packard convertible that I especially admired. It was
turquoise blue and had a rumble seat. He sold it to me for
thirty-five dollars because he was getting in some new
classics and needed the space.

I had a gig in Miami and I also wanted to work the
GiGi Room at the then brand new Fontainbleau Hotel.
Jackie Gleason was doing his musical telecasts in Florida
and I wanted to work for him, too. I decided to go by car
because I planned to stay in the Miami area and get lots
more jobs once I was there, so I'd needed wheels. Renting
a car once I was there would be insanely expensive in season: cabs were few and far apart. Forget buses: they only
ran in the daytime. So I started for Miami Beach and
that's when my snazzy convertible revealed itself as the
gas guzzler of all time. I got there, but most of my money
was left in gas station cash registers on the way. I arrived
nearly broke.

My gig was with Alan Gale, a very successful comic
who owned his own club in Miami. He always booked a
male singer for the whole season. It was a beautiful place
and I really had a good time there.

In the meantime, I met a man named Milton Wall, a
retired real estate man who wanted to be an agent. He
heard me sing and told me he could get me other engage-

ments. He liked me and I liked him. He could talk paint off the walls. We agreed he would be my Miami Beach agent and I told him I wanted to do the GiGi Room.

After that gig ended, I was soon poor again. Now the Miami Beach gas stations had my money. Luckily I was staying rent free in a friend's condo in Coral Gables. There was a pool. It was a lovely place. An older couple took me in like family and when I was out of money, fed me great meals. He was Jewish and very ill. She was Irish and spry, full of energy. I would regale them with tales of show business and when dinner was over, we'd watch TV together and just hang out.

So, once again down to my last couple of bucks, I went to the Five & Ten and bought a pretty candle in a candleholder as a gift to my dear neighbors. I told myself, this is the way of the Law of Prosperity. I will spend all I have and it will come back to me. I gave the gift to my friends and they loved it. At five P.M. that very day, I got the call to come and work on the Jackie Gleason TV show in Fort Lauderdale. The Law of Prosperity had worked again!

Jackie's TV show was produced in Miami because Jackie lived in Fort Lauderdale where the golf was year round and he refused to work in New York or Hollywood. So while I visualized working for him, I discovered that Lyn Duddy, a writer I'd done an industrial show with in New York, was a writer on the Gleason show. He was good at writing lyrics fast, to suit situations. I got in touch with him and said I'd like to work with him on the Gleason show. He said he'd try to find something for me.

Visualizing includes a lot of work. Did I mention that before? If I didn't, I should have. Finding out who was working on the Gleason show took time and research, but it paid off. As I said, I got the call. Jackie and his company

185

were doing shows based on the countries of Europe. They'd be doing one on Italy, and Lyn needed someone who knew Italian, to help him write lyrics and dialogue. I gave him Italian words to fit whatever he needed. Then Lyn put me in the show, playing an Italian character. I got along well with everyone and it worked out fine. We did one-hour musical comedies, with dancing, singing and plot lines, every week. Fantastic! I had worked before with June Taylor, who, with her troupe, did all the dance numbers. Her assistant, Peter Gladke, and I had worked together in a number of shows. He was a fabulous choreographer. He always liked my work, so he pushed for me, too. I did practically a whole TV season on the Gleason show.

Meanwhile, I did my usual metaphysical routine, going to the Fontainebleau in the late afternoons for coffee, then walking through the ground floor to the GiGi Room, the current object of my visualization. I learned the routine of the staff, who set up every afternoon at the same time. One day I walked up on the bandstand and stood there, visualizing what it would look like when I performed there, tables covered, china and silver and crystal laid, customers arriving, ordering, chatting. Then I visualized the band behind me, the room going quiet. Then I sang, *a capella*.

The staff went on about its business. Some of them smiled.

Milton Wall was working the phones with his contacts, schmoozing with the boys and doing the usual agent things to get me a job. Between my visualizing and his schmoozing, I got the job! I opened at the "World Renowned GiGi Room" to rave reviews.

Why wasn't I happy?

This time "they" came to the GiGi Room, in a group of

people who had a late dinner, applauded me politely and left after the show.

At that time, my life was a blur of club dates, TV shows, rehearsals with new accompanists and orchestras, constant travel, and I hated it all. I was lonely. I believed my talent was drying up, endlessly singing the same songs in the same way with the same arrangements to the same audiences. Only the scenery changed. My time at the Conservatory and the early years in the business had been one of growth, of learning my craft and using it to entertain in very different places, with vastly different audiences. I had, to put it simply, loved what I was doing. Now I hated what I was doing. I hated myself and I doubted my talent would survive another month of dreary, smoke-filled rooms, singing to people who had heard it all before and never cared anyway. I had stopped developing and was working only from the surface. I was turning into what I despised, a man who had reached a plateau and was stuck on it, earning a great living, but afraid to give it up and go back to New York and learn to connect with the feelings in my music, so I could love doing it again.

I looked out at the glorious view from the window of my lush suite and said to myself, "You're in a dangerous depression, you're lonely, you're unfulfilled. You have to visualize what you really want to do and go for it. You must go back to New York City and take classes in musical comedy, stage movement, dancing, acting and voice. You've always made a living. You can do this. You *must* do this! It will be hard but it is absolutely necessary to find the way to get to your emotions, put them into your voice and performance. Then you'll enjoy your talent again."

That was the night a man called "J.R." came into the GiGi Room and invited me to have a drink with him after

187

the last show. He told me he represented a group of people who liked to back talent, not with handouts but with jobs in venues they owned. I told him what I wanted to do: go to New York and work there so I could study and save my professional life.

Nothing more was said. I was smart enough by then not to ask who these men were. I went back to New York, worked in their clubs and others, earned enough to pay for classes, pay the rent and eat. I was never introduced to these men, never spent time with them. J.R. would call and say, "I've got a job for you," and tell me where and when.

I hadn't fooled my mother at all. She did not hide her disapproval of me, no matter how I explained it to her.

It was a measure of the depth of my despair that night in the Fontainebleau Hotel that I would endure her anger and her unrelenting repetitions of the unpleasant things that could happen to me if I put a foot wrong with "them."

When J.R. retired, another man became their liaison with me, until he died. I went to his funeral. I never heard from "them" again.

My mother was relieved, and so was I.

Eddie Fisher

I was doing the late show in a Miami club. The orchestra was good, I had a first rate pianist and the audience was attentive. We were well into "The Shadow Of Your Smile," a beautiful song from *The Sandpipers,* a movie starring Elizabeth Taylor and Richard Burton.

Into the club, across the stage, up to the piano staggered an extraordinarily drunk Eddie Fisher, newly divorced from Miss Taylor. He snatched the music from the piano and proceeded to tear it to shreds and drop them on the floor. Then he turned away and sat down in a corner, nice and quiet.

The audience was surprised, horrified and curious to see if the pianist and I would survive this sneak attack. I was all of the same. We made it, without a break, to wild applause. After the show, I walked up to Mr. Fisher and said, "That was disrespectful. You sabotaged my act." He stared at me, glassy-eyed, for a brief moment, then blinked. He either didn't care or he didn't understand. I saw this behavior as an omen of things to come and took "The Shadow of Your Smile" out of the show. With any luck, no more drunks would do star turns during my numbers. And it was my last night in Miami.

Two Near Death Experiences

In 1940, I almost died. It's a miracle I'm here. Then again, in 1993, I almost died again. I feel like a cat with only seven lives left.

The first time, I was sixteen and a champion runner. I had medals and cups for running. So when I felt an occasional pain, I thought it was just from running. I would feel it on my left side, not my right, which is where your appendix is supposed to be. It wasn't anything really bad. It wasn't real PAIN pain. It was just a little twinge.

One night in late October, after I had gone to bed, my whole body erupted in agony. I was a volcano. It was the most horrible pain I had ever experienced. It felt as if I had been shot. My body imploded. That's how it felt. Oh, my God. My bedroom was at the back of the house. My parents were still up in the living room. It was a long way off. I could hear their voices. I couldn't speak, shout or scream. I couldn't do anything. Finally I was able to get out some sound and they came running. Well, I thought they were going to die. They called our family doctor, bundled me up and put me in the car. He said he would meet us at the hospital. When I got there, I had no readable temperature, it was so high. They got me ready for an operation and they didn't really know what they were looking for. Finally they located my appendix on the left side. It had ruptured and peritonitis had set in. They had to put in drainage tubes to drain the infected pockets. There were no sulfa drugs, no penicillin then. I woke to discover I had two tubes in my abdomen and I said, "Oh, God, no." About a week later, they said, "We've got to go in again." I needed more draining. Then a few days after that, they had to do it again. I was doing all right until they mentioned that last one and I thought, *Oh, Jesus!*

I had the most fantastic nurses when I was in that hospital. Those people were just wonderful to me. One was a really attractive, zippy young woman and she would talk to me about her boyfriend, Jim. So I used to sing to her, "Jim never ever brings me pretty flowers." The other nurse was Virginia Revers. When she wasn't busy during the night, she would sleep with her head on my bed. She was unbelievably kind. When I used to get really down, Virginia and the younger nurse, Jane, would stage baby powder fights in my room. I couldn't laugh because it hurt too much, but it took my mind off the pain for a while.

Virginia and I stayed friends until she died. She became a radiologist for a doctor in Buffalo after she left the hospital. Little did she know what that was doing to her body. She wound up with every illness you can imagine from the radiation. Everything went wrong. She had married a wonderful man but her life was shortened. She died in her late fifties, really quite young. It was too bad because she was so great. I never forgot her.

I was in a two-bed room. My room mate was one of the most wonderful men I've ever met. He was the head of a big company. You never saw so many flowers, so many people coming to visit. He was Catholic, too, and very religious in a spiritual way. I was reminded of him not long ago by a man from Chase Manhattan. They had the same look of command. My room mate was loving and giving. Every time I went to the operating room, he would pray for me the whole time I was there. As I was rolled out, he would take out his rosary and pray. It was beautiful. He was there almost the whole time I was. We just hit it off. I couldn't understand his wife's attitude. She wasn't nice to him, always putting him down. All this behavior happened as he got better. By the time I left, he and I were good friends.

So my parents, my nurses and my room mate came through for me. It was a matter of life or death and they knew it. My mother had something else on her mind. When they first took me to the operating room, she challenged our family doctor, who was bald. Mother said to him, "If you don't save my son's life, I will tear every piece of hair out of your head!" He said, "I don't have any hair." She said, "I don't care!" That was so like my mother.

Another special thing I remember from that time was charlotte russe, the pastry made of lady fingers and whipped cream. When they finally let me eat, it was the only thing I wanted. The aunt who had gotten most of my grandfather's money would sneak them to me. I think that's why my parents finally forgave her.

I got out of the hospital on Thanksgiving morning. I'll never forget it. Every Thanksgiving, for me, there's such a feeling of remembrance about that whole episode, and how grateful I was that I could leave the hospital, and that I was alive.

It wasn't until the first of the following year, 1941, that I was able to go back to school. My friends on the block brought me homework and I managed to get through. I didn't lose any time and was able to graduate with my class.

After that Christmas, my room mate invited me to his house for dinner. There were a couple of children. His wife was not happy that I was there. She was in a bad mood that whole evening. It was the most uncomfortable dinner I'd ever had. I had so looked forward to it. He was disturbed by it, too. I wasn't able to keep the friendship going. I wasn't smart enough or old enough to know I could have called him at work, seen him for lunch. He was such a wonderful man. We had really connected. His wife didn't seem to appreciate him. Or maybe it was me she didn't appreciate!

For a time I couldn't support my voice properly because of the continuing pain and sensitivity of my belly muscles. I always favored that side until years later when I found out that the muscles had become just as strong as every where else. When I was eighteen, in 1942, the draft board rejected me when they got a look at my scars. But I was glad to do "Armed Forces Mail Call." It made me feel I was able to do my part in the war effort.

I acquired an outlook on life that was different from that of other sixteen-year-olds that I knew. I had found out what was important to me: singing. I decided that was what I was going to do. I think it accounts for my not being driven. I was determined, but not in the way I might have been. When you're sixteen, lying in bed, in terrible pain, you come to a lot of conclusions because you really think about death. So in that sense I guess all my ambition and aggression went into knowing that what meant more to me than anything was singing, that I had to do it, I had to put all my energies into it. I had been doing that already, but not with that clear realization. I never felt rushed after that. Where would I be rushing to? I enjoyed every minute, every day. I knew that you don't know when it will all end. I no longer felt that teenage conviction that nothing could kill me. It made me grow up fast. I wonder if I was ever young. When I think about it now, I see that I always had feelings about other people. I knew my grandparents were very lonely on the farm. It could be desolate out there in winter. It was important for me to spend time with them even though I felt lonely at times, missing my family and my friends. I would spend hours in the upstairs bedroom, sitting on a window seat and reading. But I wanted to be with them. I knew they wouldn't be there forever.

My second brush with death happened on Christmas morning in 1993. I was driving to Buffalo with John Harris, Giacomo (my dog) and a trunk full of Christmas presents. We were on the New York Thruway. There was no snow. It was a perfect trip on a perfect day and I had just checked my rear view mirror and said to John, "Isn't this amazing? There's no one on the road," when out of nowhere a car came barreling along and it must have been going over a hundred miles an hour. It plowed right into me on the driver's side and we spun around three times, bouncing off the concrete barrier every time. It was just horrible. John caught poor Giacomo as he was going through the windshield and held on to him for dear life. Giacomo was too frightened to bark. Fortunately, my car was a Mercedes Benz. It was a wonderful car. If you're going to have an accident, have it in a Mercedes Benz! Without the airbags, the seatbelts, the strong frame, we would all have been killed or permanently disabled.

The driver of the speeding car was a boy who had been up all night, drinking.

It was such a tremendous shock, a bolt of lightning, just like the first time, when my appendix ruptured. I was so upset about the car, I cried. John tells me I said to him, "Oh, my beautiful car! I worked all my life so I could have a Mercedes Benz!" It was demolished.

Deepak Chopra writes about detachment, the importance of detachment from things. He says it so simply and concisely, you can understand it quickly. He teaches the importance of detachment from any THING: that table, the piano, this house, anything. I'm not as detached as I should be, but since that disaster, I'm not preoccupied with owning a Mercedes Benz. I drive an SUV, a Toyota Previa, and it's great.

Murder

I was living and teaching on West 73rd Street, around the corner from Riverside Drive. Very early, famous students came there for private lessons and classes. The neighbors never complained, I think because they loved sharing a staircase with stars. Even the non-stars were gorgeous.

An attractive woman had moved into the fourth floor apartment at the top of the stairs. She was young, peppy, had a little bit of an attitude. She was teaching at a Catholic school on the East Side, the one Jackie Kennedy Onassis' children attended. We used to speak, but no more than pleasantries.

I had a habit of opening my door and letting my dog, Golden Boy, run ahead of me as I went down to get the mail. I'd leave the apartment door open and he would race me up the stairs and run inside. He always won.

This particular afternoon, about two o'clock, I opened my door and saw a young man coming down the stairs. As he passed me, I felt a chill. Something wasn't right about him. Just then Golden Boy came running up. The young man looked at me from across the hall. I stepped back inside, taking Golden Boy with me, and locked the door. I went to a window and watched. He had turned toward Riverside Drive. Then he was gone.

An older woman lived directly upstairs from me. She had a dog, too. I felt I had to go up and check on her. Then

I went up to the fourth floor where the school teacher lived. Her door was slightly ajar. I didn't touch it. I went down to my apartment and got on with my day.

About four, there was a knock on my door. It was our super with two plainclothes detectives. They asked me if I had seen any strangers in the building. I asked them what had happened. They told me the teacher had been murdered in her apartment. Stupidly, I blurted out, "I saw the man!" I told the detectives I was teaching all day and wouldn't be finished before nine P.M. They said, "We'll be back." Don't ask me why they didn't say, "Forget it. You're coming with us," but they didn't.

The rest of my students came through the crowd that gathers when police and press arrive anywhere in New York. Maybe the people thought we were making a movie. My mind was at sixes and sevens. The class was stunned when I told them what had happened.

From that day on, my life was hell. I begged the detectives to keep my name out of the papers and they did. They had my undying, literally, gratitude. Then it leaked in the Sunday *Daily News,* so they gave me protection for about a week.

I went to police stations, prisons, insane asylums, looked at every mug shot in the New York area. I was the only person who knew exactly what the killer looked like and what he wore. I will never forget his eyes. And his hair was wet. His eyes blazed with energy and whatever you want to call it. I guess evil is the best word. He was young. I worked with a sketch artist and the result was an excellent likeness. He has never been caught, to my certain knowledge. I lived looking over my shoulder, scared that he'd come back for me. I moved to another apartment in a different neighborhood.

Being part of a murder investigation was about the

least fun I've ever had. I rank it now as just under my burst appendix and just above my automobile accident.

I wouldn't recognize him now, thank God.

The Late, Great Waldi

After my first Dachshund died, my first dog love, Golden Boy, I didn't want another dog. I took his death too hard. Then I met a couple on the street, a beautiful model-type woman and her ordinary looking husband. They were walking a Dachshund, and of course I stopped and said, "Oh, isn't he beautiful. I just lost my own Dachshund." They told me his name was Waldi, somehow short for Wilhelm. Occasionally I would meet them on the street and finally, one day, they said to me, "Would you mind taking care of Waldi for the weekend? We're going away and we have nowhere to leave him." I thought, I really don't want to do this. It's just too painful. I didn't know these people from Adam. But I did it. Waldi and I got along fine on the weekend.

About a month later, the husband rang my bell. He said, "We're going on a three-week modeling assignment. Would you take Waldi? We hate to put him in a kennel for that long."

I had been thinking about Waldi ever since that weekend I had with him. He was just the most wonderful dog. Different from Golden Boy, he was just sweet, with a fabulous temperament.

Well, when Waldi came up my stairs, I will never forget what he did. He walked into the apartment and he saw me and he jumped so high. I never knew a Dachshund could jump that high. He was so happy to see me. It was unbelievable. He wanted to be with me. Three weeks went by, then a month. I knew where his owners lived and I went to the building and asked if anyone had seen them. Someone said they'd moved out. *They had abandoned Waldi.*

By that time, I had just fallen in love with him. Waldi and I really loved each other and I hated to leave him at all, but we had a friend who stayed with John's animals and Waldi loved to go there and be with the other dogs while I was gone. We were going to the farm in Brocton. I can't remember why we left Waldi. I was not comfortable with the idea, I don't know why.

John had a duplex apartment. There was a spiral staircase and I was always concerned about those stairs and Waldi. We kept the stairs blocked with a kiddie gate so Waldi couldn't try to go down. Dachshunds have such short legs. Underneath the stairs were two wooden chairs.

We were out at the farm for a couple of days. Then I got a phone call, that Waldi had fallen over the railing and got spiked on a chair. I was a wreck. We left the farm in five minutes and I drove like a maniac to get to the animal hospital where he was. When I got there, they told me it was very bad but that Waldi was awake and waiting for me. They brought him out and I held him and I talked to him and he looked at me as if to say, "Oh, I'm so glad you're here. I'm so glad to see you," and he died.

I was devastated. He is buried with Golden Boy in West Hampton at the Bide-a-Wee Pet Cemetery and whenever I go there, I drive out to see them. It's the most beautiful place. It's better than any human cemetery. I feel good that Golden Boy and Waldi and my cat are buried there together. I always tell John that I want to be buried with them. Unfortunately, it's not allowed. Maybe I could sneak myself in if I'm cremated. I could ask John to dig a little hole and slip my little box in. No one would have to know. There's a stone that says, "Golden Boy, My Sweet Boy" and there's a picture of him.

All this came rushing back when I saw *Turner and Hooch*. When the dog died in that picture, after he caught the villain and Hooch was shot, it all came back, how I lost Waldi, and I cried. I thought of the awful way he died. It's very painful even at this very minute.

The Shows

Golden Apple

My first show, *Golden Apple,* opened off Broadway at the Phoenix Theater. I played Banker Parsons. *Golden Apple* had a great run at the Phoenix and moved to the ANTA Theater *on* Broadway.

It was a fascinating show to work in. The star, Kaye Ballard, and I became instant friends-for-life. Among other numbers, Banker Parsons sang as part of a quartet backing up Kaye. She took me under her wing and showed me how to be part of a big company, a new experience for me. She gave me tips on stage makeup, what to do when your costume doesn't work, how to interact with a big cast and crew, how to retain your self esteem and at the same time not step on anyone else's, so very different from clubs, television and radio. I can't tell you how much she did for me. She never treated me as less than a comrade and a good friend. Above all, she taught me a lot about how to teach by doing.

There were a lot of other fine performers in *Golden Apple* and I used to drop in to say hello to Portia Nelson and Bibi Osterwarld in their shared dressing room. One evening, Portia said, "I'd like you to meet someone. Say hello to Jane Russell." I couldn't see anyone but Portia and Bibi. Then, behind them, on a chair next to the back wall, I saw her. She had made herself invisible by simply being utterly still.

202

She didn't look at all like her screen image. Now I know that's often true of screen stars but she was one of the first I'd met. She was pleasant to me and ignored the way my jaw dropped. If she hadn't been JANE RUSSELL, I would have thought she was the American dream, the gorgeous girl next door.

I found a friend from the New England Conservatory of Music performing in *Apple*. Janet Hayes loved Mr. Whitney, my beloved teacher, as much as I did. I don't remember why she left before I graduated. We had a big reunion backstage. By that time, Janet had married the organist at the Church of Heavenly Rest in Manhattan. She later ran the York Theater company and did a lot of original material. Janet became a very important part of the New York theater community. I remember she did a show that Johnny King produced. It was a one-woman show for Vicki Stuart, told in songs of the time, about the two World Wars we have been cursed with in the 20th century. Not long after we last met, Janet died. She left me a lot of wonderful memories. I miss her.

Leave It to Jane and *Most Happy Fella*

I was late to an audition for *Leave It To Jane*. It was totally unlike me and I was quite upset. Though it was my own fault, I was able to persuade the director to let me sing after everyone else was done. It was a long wait and I was able to calm down and do a good audition. I got the part I was after, that of Stubby. The show was opening at the Sheridan Square Theater. I met more talented performers, most of them early in their careers, especially Lainie Kazan, who stood out from the rest of the cast. She was tall, beautiful, moved gracefully and had the great voice we all know now. A cast recording was made and I have a tape of it that I play now and then to remind me of those days.

Though I didn't know it at the time, a man from Frank Loesser's show, *Most Happy Fella,* was at the *Jane* audition. I'd seen *Fella* and focused on the role of Herman from that moment on. It was a tenor part and Herman sang "Standin' on the Corner" with three other tenors. Herman dominated with lots of high E's, F's and G's, what's called *tessatura* in *bel canto.* And I was a baritone. How could I do it? When *Fella* was well into its Broadway run, I was again responding to auditions. I saw one for the "Herman" role and went for it. I had worked out how I could do it. If I didn't sing a single note all day until I got on stage, I could use Herman's song as my warm-up. It worked. I sailed through the audition. The man who'd been at the *Jane* audition gave me a positive comment and I got the part. Herman liked everybody, had a cheerful, open face, and was a farmhand. I had him down cold, having worked on my grandfather's farm and picked crops for years.

Fella had some terrific performers, among them Jo Sullivan, Art Lund and Ed Steffi. When the Broadway run ended, we toured the country, playing tents and summer theaters. I did lots of advance publicity, a new experience for me.

Jo Sullivan, now Jo Sullivan Loesser, played the Mail Order Bride. We became good friends. She was and is beautiful. She was and is so talented. She's still singing magnificently. Her daughter is singing now.

Years later, when I asked Jo if we could do *Most Happy Fella* as a benefit for the Singers Forum, she said yes immediately, even though we couldn't pay the royalty. She said, "That's okay." Those are words seldom heard when the dreaded "no royalty" phrase is said aloud. This time I was supposed to play the lead, the Italian man who sends for the Mail Order Bride, but I found I couldn't teach eight hours a day and rehearse half the night, so I didn't do it. We presented *Fella* with two pianos because an orchestra was financially out of our reach. It was a big hit for the Forum. Jo came to see it and liked our format, so when she revived *Fella,* she used it with great success.

Not only is Jo singing, she's running Frank Publishing, the company her late husband, Frank Loesser, created from his glorious music. And doing it very well. I value Jo above rubies.

I remember playing Herman in a Cape Cod summer tent. We stayed there for a while and I went to Mass at the same church where the Kennedy family worshipped in Hyannisport. No one paid them much attention, but I couldn't help noticing this enormous family moving as one. This was long before they became THE KENNEDYS. In fact, I was the one who was asked for an autograph after Mass! Crazy? You bet.

Sue Ane Langdon played opposite me in *Fella.* Her character was Herman's girl friend and she was much smarter than Herman, always browbeating the poor young man for being nice to everybody. She was very talented and had good training, a fine show voice, and she moved well on stage.

I was very impressed with Sue's ability to "image" how a star lived and behaved. She always had a bowl of fresh fruit in her dressing room, a vase filled with green leaves, and it was always neat and well organized. She dressed beautifully, her hair was done every day and she was never seen without her makeup.

The rest of the cast, traveling, sleeping on buses, grew rather scruffy. We didn't have the strength to care much how we looked, except on stage. Then I found myself doing up my part of the cast dressing room, dressing well off stage. It lifted my spirits. I discovered that it assuaged some of the loneliness to keep myself presentable and prepared for any eventuality, like photographers, autograph seekers, directors and producers.

Herman learned a lot from Sue Ane after all.

Li'l Abner

I was doing "Herman" that summer in the big tent in Buffalo. It was great to be able to go home to my parents' house every night, to be fed by my mother and sisters, and they even did my laundry! My parents invited cast members and staff to dinner often. Family, friends, teachers, all came to see me. They made a claque and I got a lot of extra bows because of them.

Li'l Abner was to replace *Fella* in the tent and their advance man came to town to do his advance man things: plan the publicity, check out the facility, make sure the show could set up fast, schmooze with the tent's permanent staff, book hotel rooms for the stars and stage manager. This time he had another task. He was told to find a new Pappy Yokum. One night he came backstage and spoke to me about staying on after *Fella* closed and learning the role.

You can imagine my reaction. Me, play a "hillbilly?" After six years at the Conservatory, all my club dates and shows, my classes in modern dance and stage movement, my three languages? Whatever gave the advance man that idea?

Well, he explained, Pappy Yokum isn't that far from Herman, who is a simple country boy. He said he got a mental picture of me as Pappy Yokum the moment he saw me doing Herman. I said, "Let me think about it." There was a short silence. Then I said, "I'll do it."

So, a couple of weeks later, *Fella* moved on with a different Herman and there I was, in ragged jeans, farm boots, a torn shirt and a straw hat, doing Pappy Yokum and having an absolute ball.

Mammy Yokum was played by a wonderful character actress, Renee Riano, who had played Mrs. Jiggs in the movie version of *Jiggs*. She traveled from California in a trailer with all her cats and dogs. Renee was very supportive as I learned the role and performed it at the same time, always a hairy experience.

I had a new show for my claque to come see me in. My mother, father and sisters had a whole new cast to feed. I could stay at the house for another month.

Heaven!

I Can Get It for You Wholesale

I went into *Wholesale* when the road company started on tour. Most of the original company was in it, but not Barbra Streisand. At the time, some unrealistic (not to say crazed) persons didn't think that mattered.

The tour wasn't successful. It was a "New York" show and audiences outside the city just didn't get the Seventh Avenue humor. I had a lovely solo: "Have I Told You Lately." Streisand had pulled it all together and without her, it was going nowhere. People got tied in knots when she left the show, talking about ingratitude and stuff like that. They said the show made her a star. I said she made the show a hit.

Charlie Reilly and his comedy classes made a huge

207

deal of me getting the role, but aside from the song, I wasn't comfortable in it. I couldn't get a handle on it. It was the first and only time I was fired from anything! I was glad to be out of it. The road company of *Wholesale* closed down soon after. I was back in New York, doing classes and auditions again.

That's show business.

Great Cities

Chicago

One of the perks of singing A Big Song in *Most Happy Fella* was that I was chosen to do advance publicity for the touring company. While my fellow cast members were slogging cross-country, cheek by jowl on buses and trains, I would have been flown in ahead to do TV shows and radio interviews. I was very well treated and I did a good job of selling *Fella.*

When we were booked into Chicago, I flew in to O'Hare airport. I was to board a helicopter and go to a TV station immediately. Riding in a helicopter was to be a new experience for me. There were time issues and getting from O'Hare to anywhere was evidently difficult using surface transportation. Or maybe somebody's relative owned the helicopter company. Who knows?

I found the HELICOPTER sign. Below it sat an incredibly beautiful, smartly dressed woman, Patricia Morrison, recently starring in *Kiss Me, Kate.* I had loved her Kate. I sat down and said so, introduced myself and told her what I was doing. We just clicked. For a star of her magnitude, traveling alone even then must have been hard. There weren't the hordes of paparazzi, but fans had a tendency to assume a star wanted nothing more in life than to give them autographs, and that said star carried pen and paper just for that purpose. So a fellow performer, however unknown, must have been a relief.

We had the most wonderful helicopter ride. We exchanged addresses. Whoever was coming to collect us was late, so we talked on like bosom buddies, exchanging backstage lore and gossip. She was very religious, very Catholic. She was such a pure person, almost an ascetic and beautiful in mind and body. We wrote back and forth for years.

The next day I was again scheduled to do promotions and a car was to pick me up at my hotel. I was waiting at the curb when a shiny new limousine with a uniformed chauffeur pulled up. I thought, *For me?* and opened the door and there sat Louis Armstrong and next to him, Sessue Hayakawa, the great Japanese actor. I nearly fell into the car, mumbling my name. They smiled and nodded and went on with their conversation. I listened, trying to calm myself down. Then we all got out at the same place and went into the same studio and were booked on the same program.

Louis Armstrong was promoting his huge hit record of "Mack The Knife" from *Three Penny Opera*. He talked about his beloved agent, Abe Lastfogel. Abe had signed up Mr. Armstrong very early in his career. Their agreement was not on paper. It was a simple handshake. He was to pay Abe a thousand dollars a week, a huge amount in the early years. Whatever happened over the decades, they never had a signed agreement and always trusted one another implicitly.

Louis Armstrong laughed a lot, telling that story. He had an aura of joy about him. He was the loveliest person you could ever meet. There must have been many incidents of racist prejudice in his lifetime but he didn't reflect any shadow of prejudice himself. I thought, God, how wonderful to be that way, to keep that trust, that loyalty between two men, that acceptance of each other as equals, as brothers in their different talents.

Sessue Hayakawa was there to talk about *Bridge On The River Kwai,* the global hit movie about a Japanese prison camp in World War II. Mr. Hayakawa, for the three people who may not have seen the movie, played the Japanese officer in charge of the camp. He was nominated for (and got) an Oscar for his performance.

Although he had a little difficulty with English, he was funny and charming. I thought at the time, we Americans must seem very odd to other peoples. We spent billions of dollars and lost many wounded and dead fighting the Japanese. Then, twenty years later, having spent more billions helping them rebuild their shattered country into our industrial rival, we spend millions of dollars more to see a movie that explicitly depicts the horrors suffered by the (mostly British) prisoners in this slave labor prison camp and give the Japanese actor who epitomizes the Samurai warrior our highest accolade for his performance in the film. Inexplicable.

That day in Chicago I sang my best ever "Standin' on the Corner," from *Most Happy Fella.* I felt VERY unimportant.

New Orleans

For two hundred years, New Orleans has had a reputation as a dangerous city, wild, promiscuous, with voodoo undertones, a place to be careful in. I missed all that, but it was a great experience anyway.

I was in my late twenties when I first worked at the Monteleone Hotel. I was booked for two or three weeks, as a single. The Monteleone is at the edge of the French Quarter, a very classy hotel. While I had performed for a

211

lot of great stars, it wasn't often that they invited me to their tables, like Frank Sinatra and Sammy Davis did at the Copacabana, and introduced me to their families and friends.

Then I met Mr. and Mrs. Robert Mitchum. They invited me to sit with them between shows. They told me they loved New Orleans and came there two or three times a year. I was thrilled to listen to their stories of the crazy things that happened in the city. The waiters came to a nearby table, bearing a flaming dish. I was impressed. How naïve can you get? I said, "What is that?" Mrs. Mitchum explained crepes suzette to me. I said it sounded terrific. She said, "Why don't you have some? We'll order it." It was delicious.

Mrs. Mitchum was very natural, just like anybody's beautiful wife. Robert Mitchum was so unlike a celebrity, a famous actor, an accomplished professional, that I was bowled over. He was so real, without pretense, funny and worldly wise. The Mitchums knew New Orleans inside and out, and they loved jazz. They took me to a lot of the clubs to hear it. Jazz was new to me and it was fun.

Not too long ago, I read Shirley MacLaine's book, *My Lucky Stars*. In it she talked of her love affair with Robert Mitchum. It lasted three years. I thought they must have been a strange twosome, him so down-to-earth and Ms. MacLaine literally out of this world a good part of the time. She talked about him as a hard man to reach. He could recite poetry, the love sonnets of Shakespeare. I wouldn't have expected this very macho man to do that. In the book, she mentioned that he wanted to sing and had even made some records. That same day I saw an old movie on TV with Mitchum and Bill Holden. I was surprised to hear his voice, singing. It was a good voice. I really wish I had known that about him. I might have worked with him. Maybe he'd have had a whole new career. But I was too shy to pursue the acquaintance. His world seemed to have no connection with mine. I had only my voice and my commitment to it. Robert Mitchum had everything.

Tennessee Williams was staying at the Monteleone with his grandfather, who always seemed to be sitting in his wheelchair, alone in the lobby, always in a white suit and white straw hat. He reminded me of my own grandfather Giacomo and I sat and talked with him a number of times. Mr. Williams and his grandfather came to see me perform several times. Then he invited me to the beach with them. We would go there in his Rolls Royce, and Tennessee Williams never spoke. I was intimidated by the talent and fame of this great writer then. Now I can carry on a conversation with anybody. We'd go back to the hotel in the Rolls, he'd nod goodbye and then they'd come to see me again. Maybe it was restful having someone there he didn't have to entertain, who liked talking to his grandfather.

Years later, when I saw *Night of the Iguana,* I knew where some of his characters came from. The grandfather in the play wrote the poems his granddaughter tried to sell. He was dressed in Tennessee's grandfather's clothes, wearing his white straw hat. I'm sure Tennessee experienced the fears of starvation, hopelessness, loneliness, these two characters portrayed. What a difficult art writing is. You are your own well-spring. You must face your own pain and confusion, and use them to illuminate another place, another time, other people.

Between the Mitchums and the Williamses, New Orleans was heaven to me.

Singers Forum

John Harris and I founded the Singers Forum, but our brainchild had several godparents. When Charles Nelson Reilly asked me, "Why don't you teach?" he was godfather number one. Geraldine Fitzgerald said, "You've taught me to sing when no one else could," and became godmother number one, and then the Greek girl who introduced me to Lee Strasberg was godmother number two. Lee Strasberg demonstrated complete faith in me based on our first and only discussion: he turned over the new voice and speech departments to me and became godfather number two.

The eighteen years with the Lee Strasberg Institute were a postgraduate experience in every aspect of the voice. Producing a good voice involves the use of the whole body. Physical strength and awareness of one's own emotions are the basic tools of a singer. Musicality and discipline are givens. Everything else flows from these essential ingredients. Students came from everywhere on the strength of Lee's name and reputation. I was being overwhelmed by sheer numbers, teaching both voice and speech. I had to get help or go under.

Then I met John Harris. A classical baritone, a Juilliard graduate, he had lost his voice while touring Europe with a European opera company. He was depressed and desperate. I offered him a private lesson, and I was sure I could help him. Then we worked through a whole night on a stage at the Institute. I led him through the basics of

Mr. Whitney's *bel canto* which simply means "beautiful singing." It's a scientific approach to the voice that teaches the student how to breathe, how to properly support the sound, how to prevent any pressure on the throat area and to project the sound into the resonators that give the vibrations that make one's own distinct sound. The voice never gets tired. It doesn't wear out. It doesn't get hoarse. The sequence is, breathe in to fill the lungs completely, almost like inflating a tire. Learn to keep the diaphragm and the belly muscles firm. This is the beginning of muscle development. Keep the belly muscles firm, going up to or down from a high note. Take air from the supply and let it travel up from the lungs and through the vocal cords. The chest moves up and the chin tips slightly down so that the air can hit all the resonators around the face and head. This produces a sound that's very beautiful, strong, healthy and can last. It's all done through the body and, of course, the mind. About eight hours in, he was able to sing a whole scale, perfectly. In his joy, he cried and so did I, in relief. We have been close friends ever since. He had the most beautiful speaking voice (and still does, by the way) so after checking with Lee, I gave him the speech classes. If this isn't a perfect example of "You get by giving," (another way of describing the Law of Prosperity) I don't know what is. He needed my help and I gave it to him, without any expectation of reward. Then I needed his help and he gave it, just as freely. I saved his voice and he saved my sanity!

At this time, the frameworks of voice and speech classes differed. I had a pianist who left me free to concentrate on a number of students in one class. John had no help and his students, aspiring actors all, felt free to chat, flirt, make dates and talk over auditions. John had a hell of a time getting them to work. By then he had full control of his voice and could use it like a physical weapon. He told me he knew he had a choice: walk out and stay out or dominate the class. He thought, *What shall I do?* And God told him to make the entire noisy crew lie down on the floor. He said, "GET DOWN ON THE FLOOR," in the voice that has, literally, stopped an armed mugger, turned him around and made him run. "LIE DOWN, RAISE YOUR KNEES, CLOSE YOUR EYES. BREATHE." They obeyed. He never had another wasted moment in any of his classes! We went on to combine his preparatory technique with my vocal warm-ups. We start our voice classes by instructing the class to lie down on the floor, close eyes, raise knees, breathe, and we have a simple breathing technique that opens up the lungs. The class counts to ten, starting with a breath and saying "One," going on to breathe and say, "One, two," breathe and say, "One, two, three," and so on up to a full count of ten, each separate count on its own single breath.

At some point, I was teaching classes at the Strasberg Institute, giving private lessons at my apartment, even some students at their own homes. I crisscrossed the city constantly. John was doing the same. We were wearing ourselves out. I began to visualize my dream school, a place where students would come to me. John and I stayed at the Institute for two years after Lee died. Then I realized I had to take the next step and create my own school. I had lots of teaching experience, a great reputation and very little money.

An acting teacher at the Institute, a good friend, had taken the plunge into independence and invited me to attend his classes and see the place he was working in. It was perfect, just what I wanted for myself. I spoke to John about it and he said he'd think about it. Then I decided to go out on my own, even if I didn't have a permanent place for my classes. I rented rooms in rehearsal studios and sometimes got bumped for a teacher who would pay more, or take more hours, or a show in rehearsal. I talked to my students about finding permanent space, and John did the same. Finally, a student of both of us, Robert Wall, who was a plumber by trade, said he had found a loft on lower Fifth Avenue. There was a big room that could function as both classroom and theater. We would pay about four hundred dollars a month.

Then we had to buy pianos, chairs, mikes, a sound system, phones and advertising in show business publications. We were always nearly broke, but we survived. Charlie Reilly and Geraldine Fitzgerald sent us students, many of whom were professionals before they came to us.

Johnny King originated classes in stage movement and dance. Students kept coming. Phil Campanella, Maxine Andrews' pianist and co-star, came to us with Geraldine's recommendation. Philip is now our Executive Director and has been a life-saving force for us. He'll have even more responsibilities when (and if) John Harris and I retire. Denise Galon appeared out of the blue as a student and stayed to set up a system for collecting student fees and for scheduling classes and private lessons.

Time after time, the Forum was down to it last dollar. We were rescued at critical moments by students who got jobs and caught up on their overdue accounts. We both had students who just didn't have the money but did have real talent, and we taught them for nothing. I'll never forget one student, whose life I actually saved, who had plenty of money but never paid, even though I saved her from being burned alive. She wasn't the only cheat. When we finally caught on, the cheaters would quit. We couldn't afford a lawyer to sue them in small claims court (no

Judge Judy in those days) and we didn't have time to do it ourselves.

We stayed in this space for ten years. At some point, business reasons caused Robert Wall to move out and we had the whole floor to ourselves. Then the owner of the building decided to raise the rent every year. It got higher and higher. We began to owe him money. Then he rented our floor to a martial arts school, the final blow.

Engraved on my liver is the night we were told that the Singers Forum had to leave its quarters immediately. After issuing his ultimatum, the landlord departed, taking our elevator key with him. It was embarrassing, to say the least. Our students were taking class and heard the whole discussion.

John and I stared at each other. Our faces must have resembled those of officers on the Titanic when they counted the lifeboats and found their number insufficient.

The students talked among themselves. They nominated a leader, Amy Jacobs, whose father was rich. She announced their plan. She would go to her parents and get a large check. Then she would rent a truck. The rest of the group would unhook the sound system, carry it and our few bits of furniture and such downstairs and pack it all on the truck that she would park on the street. We did all that. Then we stared at the pianos. Professional movers had brought them up, expensively. A student who had worked for a mover said, "Take off the legs and then carry the bodies down sideways." I said, "Let's do it!" and it worked.

Amy Jacobs arrived with large check and truck. It was loaded and driven to a safe place, to sit until we had a new space. The check would cover the truck and what we needed to rent another set of rooms. The next morning we found space. A lease was signed, the truck arrived and we were back in business the following day.

When I asked our students why they had done such extraordinary deeds for us, they all had the same reason: no one wanted to miss a lesson and this was the only way they could be sure of it.

Our little Titanic didn't sink.

In 1977, another godfather, Robert Malfi, appeared and suggested that we convert the Forum to a non-profit status with the Internal Revenue Service. We certainly qualified. We had no profits and were teaching students who couldn't pay, doing benefits for charities, schools and senior citizens. We went through the long and very detailed process with the Service and came out of it able to solicit and accept donations from patrons and they were tax deductible! Now we give concerts to benefit the Forum. We have work/study programs. We go to hospitals and senior citizens' nursing homes and give free performances. We took on board members who had experience with non-profit organizations and held important positions in the business aspects of show business. The pressures on me and John eased somewhat. Until 1996, we worked seven-day weeks, for the Forum and our private students. Finally, a good friend said to me, "You are working too hard. You have to cut out at least one Saturday class or you'll end up having to quit altogether." I viewed this pronouncement as a personal insult, but she didn't give up. I surrendered one class to John and felt guilty. Then one day I went to a late lunch on a Saturday when I should have been teaching, and it felt great. How right my friend was.

I gradually reduced my schedule further. I took vacations! At the same time, being me, I decided the Singers Forum needed a summer camp. We found a wonderful spot in upper New York State, S.U.N.Y. Fredonia, not far from my family's farm. It was a great experience for all of us. We've done it three times now and each year it gets better. More on this later. So my vacation became the music camp. After a while, my schedule was back to its old tricks. A few brisk discussions with my friend convinced me that I was over doing it again.

In the summer of '99, I was having a physical and the stress test was stopped after a few minutes of running. My heart was not behaving itself. My doctor, Dr. Boris Ivkov, suggested a test to discover the state of my carotid arteries. Since a blocked carotid artery had killed my dad thirty-nine years ago, I agreed. The test showed Trouble with a capital T and I was instructed by Dr. Gallucio to be at Lenox Hill hospital early the next morning, for an angioplasty. Family and friends gathered. If the reader wants to know the details of angioplasty, I refer him/her to the Web, where I am sure the procedure is conducted in its entirety, live and in color. My vote for New York's best hospital is Lenox Hill in Manhattan. The doctors were optimistic and undoubtedly capable, and aside from a big bruise on my left leg, I was back to work in a few days. Then I did the summer camp and a week of classes at Chatauqua, and finally took a vacation. The odds on my survival of that summer would not have been good if my friend had not pushed me to ease up on work and get regular checkups. I feel great. I walk briskly around my neighborhood, towed by my dear Giacomo. We are both a bit overweight and need the exercise. My diet is healthy and so is Giacomo's because he shares my every meal. I pace myself. My doctors tell me I can live to be a hundred if I behave myself. Now I seldom lose my temper and when I feel stressed, I do yoga breathing and meditate. Giacomo yawns and goes to sleep.

Over these last years, word of our school and what it offers has spread throughout the show business world. We are experiencing increasing enrollments, with many classes selling out in advance and others breaking previous enrollment records. John and I teach regularly. As the Forum continues to develop and expand, we have added extra classes to accommodate the need for a sequential course of studies for our growing student population. We now have advanced levels of instruction for speech, voice technique, performance technique. We have a popular class for both professionals and non-professionals: "Everything You Wanted to Know About Music (But Were Afraid to Ask)." Also new is our first Vocal Performance Class for children, ages eight to twelve, and a "Great Singers On Film" discussion series. Our "Jazz Improvisation Master Class" is very popular. We also have Saturday and Sunday one-day seminars covering a variety of topics related to working as a professional in the business.

Prior to the start of every term, we have an Open House. Prospective students come and visit our studios, attend sample classes, meet the faculty, ask questions (and get answers!), have refreshments and hear a short performance by students and faculty members. It's always well-attended.

The Forum gives high-quality performances year round in the evenings and on weekends. There's an "Open Mike" night on the first Friday of every month. It's a very professional cabaret setting and performers come from all over the city. The public is invited.

Community service is an integral part of the Singers Forum education. We have a City summer program, five-day clinics, as part of the New York City Sport and Arts Foundation. Our teachers travel to a different school site for each of three weeks, where they introduce city school children to the joys of musical theater. Hundreds of children come to these clinics for a wonderful time.

Our Senior Outreach and Partnership for Homeless Youth programs delight and touch people's lives in unique and meaningful ways. Several times a month, seniors in area centers, nursing homes, hospitals and hospices are treated to high quality entertainment by our troupe of volunteer performers. As the last song ends, the first question is always, "When are you coming back?" The Partnership for Homeless Youth Program is growing faster than we ever thought possible. The children experience important personal discoveries and uncover their own talents. One young girl was invited to perform on the Partnership Fall Benefit, along with opera star Jessye Norman. We are thrilled for her and wish her an extraordinary performing experience.

In the fall of '98, Phil Campanella traveled to Montreal to present a "Singing For People Who Think They Can't Sing" workshop that grew out of our first Fredonia, New York, workshop by that title, during the previous summer. John, Phil and I presented three sections of that same workshop at the Chatauqua Institute in the summer of '99. As I said, not far from my grandfather's farm, now the family's summer residence, is the town of Fredonia. It occurred to me that John and I and the Forum should explore the possibilities for using camp sites and the Music Department of S.U.N.Y. Fredonia, to bring our students from the Forum to the area for two weeks of concentrated vocal training and performance, and bring in students from Buffalo and the surrounding area at the same time. For two weeks, twenty singers gathered each week for an intensive course of instruction by our top team of professional performing artists, designed to unlock students' performance abilities in an atmosphere of total concentration. No one had family or business issues to deal with; no one's attention was diverted from the purpose of the one-week sessions for anything at all. Response to this program is so overwhelming that we had to add another week, bringing it to three weeks of immersion in the joy of performance. The gala performances given at the end of each week play to capacity audiences from the surrounding area, and the growth of each student can be measured by us from the first hesitant testing of the waters to the last bow of thanks to the audience for their standing ovations.

The original Singers Forum, tottering from payroll to payroll, rent bill to rent bill, with all the attendant hourly, daily, weekly and monthly crises, is not forgotten. John, Phil and I sometimes wonder how we survived the pressures and tensions of all those years. Mostly we reminisce about the good things, the students who moved from shy, frightened kids, afraid to sing a note in front of their first class, to the assured, talented, polished professionals so many of them have become. We have had and still have many students who don't want to sing professionally, but only for themselves, and the change that comes over them, vocally and personally, is always exciting. Business professionals learn to use their voices as part of communication in a positive way.

We are about to celebrate our twenty-sixth anniversary. We have a Web site: www.singersforum.org, and people from all over the world visit us there. The New Millennium is looking good!

Epilogue

Sicily: Visiting the Past

Our plane landed at Palermo's airport just as the rising sun lit up the terrain. We landed in a bowl, surrounded by huge mountains. I never saw colors quite like this morning's beautiful pinks and blues and greens, almost indescribable. The first look was really amazing.

What was supposed to have been a ten hour trip from New York via Rome to Palermo lasted thirty-two hours. My sisters, Annetta and Carolyn, our neighbor from Brocton, Rosemary Hayes, John Harris and myself, are all hardly in the bloom of youth, and we were exhausted.

The second impression I had of Sicily was the sight of huge mountains, ranged like teeth along the coast and covered in beautiful foliage. On the bus ride to Cinisi, where we were to stay at the Floro Park, a beautiful hotel on a peninsula outside of Palermo, for a day and night, we saw that most houses had terra-cotta tiled roofs, almost adobe-like walls with small windows, and were surrounded by lots of greenery. Sicily has its own look. I've never seen anything quite like it. So much of the Island seems to be built up on hills or along the slopes of mountains. Sicily may seem just a dot on a world map, but it's huge.

We left Cinisi the next morning to spend three days

and nights in Palermo. I had heard about the city from Grandfather Di Pasquale. We had a great time there but I found none of the places he had talked about. The fourth morning of the trip, we drove to Monte Maggiore Bel Sito, where all my grandparents were born. On the way, we went through several towns and more beautiful countryside.

We could see Monte Maggiore for miles before we got there. Bel Sito overlooks all the other towns on the mountain. The soil of the farmland surrounding it has many shades, from light to dark brown. There are more mountains on the horizon. Then we came to Monte Maggiore Bel Sito.

The town is so beautiful. The houses all have shutters and iron-work. The streets have handsome lamp posts, very simple, almost modern. We couldn't find the house where my Anselmo grandfather had lived. We passed the house on Via Garbo, where Grandfather Di Pasquale had lived with his brother and sister. I kept saying, "Bello! Bello!"

Then we went up Monte Maggiore to the top. Alongside the roadway, sheep grazed. That's where my grandfather Di Pasquali must have gone with his flocks. It wasn't very far from their house, at least not by bus, on a modern road.

A lot of families on Monte Maggiore grow grapes or flowers, and there were lemon and orange orchards further up. Their crops are sold all over Sicily. We passed a donkey pulling a heavy cart, as the road circled up the mountain and I had a flash of Grandfather and myself, with Queenie pulling the wagon load of grapes to market. These flashes occurred all the time we were in the area.

We talked about how close to the family home the sheep were grazing. Grandfather had been alone, high up on the mountain. Our translator/guide told me there were more pastures further up.

Then we went back to the house grandfather Di Pasquale had lived in and it was absolutely beautiful. A hundred years ago, the kitchen was where everybody congregated and ate. The room that's now the living room was where the family animals were kept. They had chickens in there too. I thought, *My God, this beautiful room, imagine it full of animals all winter long!* In America, we'd have torn the place down and built a new house, but not in Sicily. In Sicily, they clean it up, put in plumbing and electricity and families live in it for centuries to come. The stove grandfather described to me is still in the big room. That gave me great comfort.

We went back up to the very top of the mountain to get a panoramic view of the whole country side and as we came back down, we passed Via John F. Kennedy. It was such a simple memorial to our murdered president and I was very moved by it.

We spent wonderful hours with all kinds of relatives, Anselmos and Di Pasquales. I hated to leave.

After the trip to Monte Maggiore Bel Sito, our bus took us around the Island's perimeter. Every town, every city, was individual. One in particular, a beautiful resort right on the Mediterranean, where we stopped for lunch, really caught my eye. John and I walked to the beach afterward and a very attractive woman came out of the water, in a skimpy bikini. As we passed, she asked, "Where are you from?" I told her. She said she was from Sweden. She and her husband rent an apartment there every year, just up from the beach. In the fall, prices go way down. She said it was a comfortable place, on a street lined with elegant shops and restaurants.

Two cats were sitting on rocks surrounded by water,

sunning themselves. They must have gone out at low tide and were content to wait for the low tide before going ashore. They were very comfortable.

In this town, my cousin has a summer place. His family spends every August there. They want us to come and visit. I'd like that. Our interpreter/guide was a dynamic woman, one of those great people you meet who can do anything. She solved all our problems. Most women her age in Sicily don't go out to work. They are family-oriented and two or three generations live in the same house. They all seem to get along. One of another cousin's daughters, the younger, works in Palermo, has her own apartment in the family building and goes there weekends. The older, in her late thirties, is a teacher. She told me education is very important in Sicily. The children do their homework, and their parents don't have to hound them over it. A couple of teenagers visited with us for a while. Then they stood up and said they had to go home to do their homework. No fuss, no arguments. They respected their parents and listened to them.

We visited a town of Greek origin, with famous mosaics that have been preserved for many centuries. We walked around on platforms and looked down at them. They were hauntingly lovely. And they hadn't been taken to "safety" like the so-called "Elgin Marbles." A huge concert was going on, starring a very famous African singer, and that night the town was absolutely packed with people and cars.

The next day John and I were in shorts and it turned out to be the one day it really rained on the whole trip. We were wet and shivering. There was a little shop nearby and we ordered cappuccino to warm up. One girl took our order. Another girl came out from the back to serve us. She was absolutely stunning. I thought, *Ye gods, where did she come from?* It was that kind of shock. I don't think she had any idea that she was stopping traffic. She spoke in a very small "Marilyn Monroe" voice. I had the feeling of being in an Italian movie where a producer walks in and signs up the waitress on the spot to a contract to star in a black and white movie about World War II.

A weather word about Sicily: bring a lightweight rain jacket with a hood. Just roll it up and stick it in your bag. Mornings were clear. After lunch there would be a drizzle of rain and it would get cold. It keeps everything looking green, and your teeth chattering. Socks are a must.

Taormina was a paradise: scents of flowers, pure, clear air, fabulous hotels built on the sides and on the top of a mountain.

Greeks, Romans, Scandinavians and Moors arrived in Sicily over centuries, to leave their mark on the Island and its people. Some are dark-skinned, with dark eyes and hair. There are a lot of blondes with blue eyes and redheads with green eyes. The churches and public buildings are beautiful, city streets narrow. I loved every inch of the Island and every person I met.

I had a very warm, loving feeling all the time I was in Sicily. I didn't feel at all a stranger. It felt like I was part of the place. I laughed all the time. It was a very happy experience. I loved most walking into the house where my grandfather Di Pasquale had lived. That was very special. I felt very close to him the whole trip. I could see him in his house. The sight of the old stove moved me so. His family and their animals all lived in that house. I kept on thinking of him all the time.

My cousins told me what happened to Grandfather Di Pasquale's share of the family property. I had been told that the local priest talked him into signing it over to the church. Not true. Maybe his family bought it from him and he used that money to buy his land in Brocton. Cousin Rose's mother ended up with the Monte Maggiore Bel Sito property. I don't know what happened after she died, but would love to find out. I think Grandfather's nephews and nieces took it over. The woman who lives there now is not a relative. She bought it from whoever had it after Rose's mother died. Even she seemed to be a person from the past. She acted and spoke and looked the way my grandfather's generation did.

Seeing Sicily in 1999 made me wonder why my grandparents left so beautiful a land to come to America without anything much but their bare hands, to start a whole new life. I finally realized that a hundred years ago, Sicily must have been poverty stricken and lawless. Far away, America would have seemed a beautiful dream. When they got here, they must have been shocked by the reality of 1900s America, but it never occurred to them to go back to Sicily.

It never occurred to me, until I went to Sicily, that I must have built my personal, positive philosophy on my grandfather's move to America. It was his dream. He worked to get his dream place. He lived a good but hard life, finding his land and keeping it during the bad times, always with the vision that his only child, my mother, would have the farm when he died. Having a dream and working to achieve it was my grandfather's gift to me.

You can achieve anything if you dream big enough. You have to visualize that dream. Then you've got to work hard to attain your dream. If you do, you begin to attract all the right things to yourself, to produce that dream. If you want to become a singer, a great singer, you can, if you dream big enough and work hard enough. It's all up to you. It's all up to your mind and body.

You can't let anything distract you from that positive road that's taking you where you want to go. You have to be an eternal student in this business. The creative process goes on all the time. As you age and as you change, as you grow, everything in your mind and body has to be dealt with in a different way. You can never stop learning how to sing. You can never stop learning how to become a better performer. There's no end to it. That's what has made my life so exciting.

I'm so glad I went to Sicily, and I'm going again soon. I feel so at home there.

About the Author

Andy Anselmo was born in Buffalo, New York, and studied voice at what is now Buffalo's Community Music School, financing his studies by delivering newspapers at dawn each morning. During World War II he did a full-time program for Armed Forces Radio while attending Canisius College in Buffalo. From there, he attended the New England Conservatory of Music in Boston, where he won scholarships, took on odd jobs to support himself, and learned the secrets of the *bel canto* technique, from the great William L. Whitney, that would serve the author well in his career. The author began, and continues to enjoy, a long, distinguished, and satisfying career teaching voice to professionals all over the world, culminating with his founding of the Singers Forum in New York City. *A Star-Crossed Life: A Memoir* is the story of his wonderful journey.

—*Stanley F. Druckenmiller*